Ayalla Reuven-Lelong

RIDING THE WHITE WATER RAPIDS

*The Story Of My Success At **KPMG***

Ayalla Reuven-Lelong

RIDING THE WHITE WATER RAPIDS

*The Story Of My Success At **KPMG***

Ayalla Reuven-Lelong

RIDING THE WHITE WATER RAPIDS
The Story Of My Success At KPMG

Second Edition

Editor: **Ilan Reuven-Lelong**
Translator: **Tom Dolev**
Cover and Book Design: **Studio Dor Cohen**

Copyright © 2020 by Ayalla Reuven-Lelong and EQ-EL

Notice: This book is a revised and amended, special edition of the book by the same author: Riding the White Water Rapids: *Career Success in the 21st Century (Special Accountants› Edition)*, Published by Contento Now (2015).

Printed in Israel, January 2020

I dedicate this book to the leaders and employees at KPMG all over the world, who work relentlessly, passionately, and purposefully to inspire confidence and empower change, creating a better world for all of us.

Table of Contents

Foreword by Tom McGinness
Co-Chair Global KPMG Enterprise Family Business
and Head of Family Business,
KPMG in the UK

Our Workplaces are rapidly changing, and many scholars and experts claim that we are in the midst of one of the most significant revolutions in organisational history, some say the most dramatic one. Among the factors that are driving this change are; a fast-evolving world of technology, heavy regulation, the new Y and Z generations, and our clients who have become more and more sophisticated and demand more value from us. These changes will have major implications for every aspect of our work, from our business models to our organisational culture, our ability to become the clear choice in the market and our personal lives.

On an organisational level, to continue and survive and even strive in the ever-changing reality, regardless of the industry they operate in, organisations will need to reinvent themselves, their culture, services, products and business models. This is probably the only way to stay relevant and develop a winning value proposition to all the stakeholders: employees, clients and the society at large. On a more personal level, to continue and succeed in today's competitive job market, in which change is the only constant, it is certain that at some point we will all have to reinvent ourselves professionally.

Last year, when I was introduced by Ayalla to the Five Lands Model, in our annual Enterprise Conference, it immediately resonated with what I thought we, as partners, auditors, consultants and advisors, will need in order to stay relevant in the markets and provide our clients and employees with a winning value proposition. The Five Lands Model is an inclusive conceptual framework of the set of skills that will help all of us at KPMG to deal successfully with our current and future challenges and make our clients and employees see the difference in us. Moreover, this journey provides us with the ability to invent and reinvent ourselves personally and professionally.

From my point of view, embarking on this journey will be beneficial for all of us at KPMG on three different levels. The first one is our ability to lead in the market over our competition and become the clear choice. Much like the challenges we are confronting, our clients are also challenged by the same white-water rapids. Rightfully, they expect us to bring more value and help them to sustain their success in the long run. They expect us to understand their challenges, businesses and business environments. They also expect us to understand the global and local trends that may influence or impact their success and to bring them innovative solutions. Moreover, they need us to help them develop their organisational ability to adapt and evolve in a rapidly changing world.

Our clients need us to really connect with them on an emotional level too and have high expectations from all of us at KPMG, and we all have to do our very best to take these seriously and strive to act on them. To do so, each and every one of us needs to see himself or herself as a one-person startup and invest time and effort to find opportunities to learn more, discover more and develop a new set of skills. The Five Lands models' abilities and skills are at the heart of our ability to make our clients see a difference in us and become the clear choice.

The second level is our ability to provide a winning value proposition to our employees. Gone are the days when companies provided lifelong employment in exchange for loyal service. This employment model, which was good for many years, belongs to the era of stability. Today, employees expect us to create a winning culture in which they will feel respected, empowered and meaningful. They want us to help them grow and flourish, and to invest in their personal development and career. We, as the leaders, must develop a new mindset and a new set of skills and become an inspirational leader. To do so, we first need to think differently and realise that "what we have always done" doesn't work anymore when it comes to our relationships with our employees. Then we have to hold a growth mindset attitude, to be more creative and innovative and to develop our emotional intelligence. By doing so, we are going to gain the hearts and minds of our employees, and in return, they will help our company to grow and flourish.

The competitive advantage of the 21st century lies in the company's culture and the ability of the leaders to inspire their employees. Putting the time and effort to go through the Five Lands Journey will help all of us to become inspiring leaders, who gain the hearts and minds of our employees.

The third level of the benefit that this journey offers is our personal lives, as individuals, spouses and parents. The pace of change does not influence us only in our professional lives. In many ways, it influences us even more in our personal lives. To be content in an ever-changing and high complexity reality we will need to know ourselves better, effectively adapt to changes, have better interpersonal relationships, become better parents, make better life choices, and maintain better well-being.

And, as a final point, I would like to note that this journey doesn't end with our own development as partners. One of our main tasks as such is to support our employees in the same journey, guiding and helping them to upskill themselves so that they are better equipped to reinvent themselves for the future.

**

'Riding the White-Water Rapids: The Story of My Success at KPMG' – is a special version that Ayalla has created especially for us at KPMG. This version is uniquely written to suit the culture, language and notion of our firm. I have no doubt that each and every one of us will find himself or herself in this story.

Tom McGinness

Introduction

For the past twelve years, I've been serving as a consultant for KPMG. I have been involved in the design and implementation of many of the firm's strategic processes that were led by senior partners, which include: becoming an Employer of Choice; Talent Management (People Strategy); building Client Service Teams; and being the Trusted Advisor of the company's C-suite and providing them a winning value proposition (Growth Strategy). My work targeted the development of soft strategies within employees, leaders and senior management in order to create a culture of a growth mindset and to prepare the firm towards continued success in our fast-changing reality.

During this period of time I witnessed the overwhelming change the accounting profession was going through, which fundamentally changed the rules of the game and, therefore, the role of leadership within the firm. The factors that propelled this revolution include globalization, extensive regulation, technology, the emergence of Generation Y, fragile sustainability and fierce competition for clients who demand higher value and quality services for a lower price. It actually became evident to all of us at KPMG that what we used to call 'soft skills' became the 'hard stuff.' This is also why what we used to call 'soft skills' are now often referred to as 'critical skills,' and this is also how we view them in this book. While in the past the criteria for success and promotion to leadership positions were mainly related to professional expertise (quality), in the present organizational reality, employees and leaders are required to have a far more complex range of skills, particularly a significant amount of critical skills related to the firm's people and growth strategy. Unfortunately, those who do not internalize this reality will find themselves irrelevant to the market and, eventually, to the firm.

Throughout my journey towards understanding what the accountants and advisors of the 21st century need in order to succeed in the turbulent reality we all are now facing worldwide, I delved into the leading research and professional literature on the subject. I studied the various models and applied them to the daily practice at different departments in the firm. In my lectures and personal meetings, I had conversations with hundreds of employees, managers, directors, partners and experts from various fields. Eventually, these led me to an understanding of the most important competencies and skills that distinguish between those who are capable leaders in the gushing "white waters" and those who are not, as portrayed in the Five Lands model we have created.

I decided to write this book as an imaginary story, since over the past few decades serving as a consultant, I had discovered that we learn best and are most willing to change our mindset when hearing stories that are connected to our personal and professional world. In fact, stories helped me connect with the leaders I worked with on an emotional level and helped me convey key messages in a way that they would remember and would help them take action and cultivate the competencies and skills necessary in order to maximize the potential hidden in each and every one of them. The book 'Riding the White Water Rapids – The Story Of My Success At KPMG,' is an accumulation of my knowledge and expertise combined with my consulting experience at KPMG.

***

The first part of this book is the story of a classic talented and ambitious director at KPMG, Michael. Although he excels professionally, Michael is forced to realize that the times were indeed changing. Following a discouraging annual feedback meeting, he is suddenly confronted with the reality that he must make a different kind of effort in order to maintain a successful career and help KMPG achieve the firm's vision of becoming the clear choice for clients and the most talented employees. In order to ensure his continued success, Michael has to set out on an unusual journey, escorted by an intelligent, pleasant and assertive consultant named Rona who will guide him through the five lands.

In each land, Michael will meet different people, some of them quite strange and surreal. Through these experiences, he will gather insights that are indispensable for his continued success in the 21st century at KPMG.

The second part of the book contains questions for thought and reflection, in addition to numerous theories and research upon which the book's chapters are based.

It is important to emphasize that even though the protagonist of the story is a director, this book is also intended for employees who are not yet leaders or are not interested in management positions. It is intended for all of those who are interested in recognition and ongoing success in their careers, while still enjoying life to the fullest, including family, friends and leisure.

Some of you will be satisfied with simply reading Michael's story, while others will also wish to delve into the book's theoretical parts. Either way, I wish you the best of luck on your personal journey.

***

Like the white water rapids that serve as a metaphor for today's reality, the concepts covered in this book evolve faster than we can write about them – the journey to success and fulfillment is a never-ending adventure. I will be happy to receive your feedback on this book: suggestions, questions or comments. You are welcome to write to me at *ayalla@eq-el.co.il*.

Also, my LinkedIn profile name is 'Ayalla Reuven-Lelong'.

Acknowledgments

I would like to acknowledge all those who helped me during my personal journey and made the writing of this book possible. Most of all, I would like to acknowledge all the leaders whom I had the privilege to accompany during the last few years. Openly and dedicatedly, they enabled me to gain valuable insights into the quest for success in this radically dynamic reality that we are currently experiencing.

To **Professor Ilan Meshulam** (Former Head of the School of Management of Haifa University and former Co-CEO of Intel Israel), thank you so much for being our mentor in my teams' journey. Thank you for sharing with us your precious experience as a leader and as a researcher. You are a true source of inspiration to all of us.

Special thanks to **Eran Shalev** (Senior Partner at KPMG Israel) who, through his unique approach and personality, challenged me and helped me learn and understand the complexity of the world of leadership in our fast-changing reality. Thank you for enabling me to create and implement the Five Lands model.

To **Jonathan Lavender** (Global Chairman, KPMG Enterprise), thank you for being a very significant partner in my personal journey through the world of accountants and advisors. From you, I learned what true passion and devotion to each and every client means. Thank you for your guidance and illuminating insights.

To **Ramona Jurubita** (Senior Partner, KPMG Romania), thank you for being the first pioneer to lead the departmental process at KPMG Romania. Thank you for your contagious enthusiasm, your courage to try new paths, your partnership, and commitment to the departmental process, eye-opening insights, sincerity and depth.

To **Maria Stancu** (Marketing Director at KPMG Romania), thank you so much for seeing the true potential of our mutual journey much before I saw it myself. Thank you for your creativity, wonderful ideas and genuine optimism throughout the different stages of the process.

To **Dr. Niva Dolev**, my friend and partner, thank you for the infinite consultations and for your depth, insights, encouragement, empathy and support throughout the years, which I do not take for granted. Thank you for making me a better professional time and time again.

To my partner **Ilan**, the man who is always with me, a huge thank you for your unending support and giving, your special way of thinking, your illuminating questions, your infinite depth and your oh-so-special ability to make everything I do better and more meaningful.

I wish to thank all those whose ideas and models are described in this book. Much effort was made to avoid reproduction of copyrighted material and to present these works in a manner that constitutes fair use. Above all, I hope this book reflects my great appreciation of these works. I encourage readers to delve further and read the cited sources, as they are all essential readings for anyone interested in succeeding in the 21st century.

Ayalla Reuven-Lelong, January 2020

Leaders in the New Era of the Workplace: Are You Dying Slowly?

Based on the Work of Pablo Neruda
(Nobel Prize Winner in Literature, 1971)

You Start dying Slowly as a Leader

When you do not find the courage to step daily out of your comfort zone;
If you pursue perfection and don't understand that failure is not the opposite of success but part of it;
When you don't feel comfortable in the uncomfortable;

You Start dying Slowly as a Leader

If you do not use your intuition, imagination, and creativity daily;
If you don't have worthy challenges, those which make your eyes sparkle and shine, and your heart dance to the beat of an unfamiliar drum;
When you do not risk what is safe today for the uncertainty of tomorrow;

You start dying slowly as a Leader

When you don't pay attention to your own emotions and to those of others;

If you do not appreciate and accept yourself as a positive and talented professional;

If you don't build new relationships, based on deep trust;

When you become a disciplined slave of your own ideas and habits, walking every day and every hour on the same paths;

If you lose your curiosity, passion, and determination to be the best person in the room;

You start dying slowly as a Leader

If you cannot feel a sense of higher purpose in your daily work;

If you lose your hope and optimism;

If you don't have a few people around you to support you on a rainy day;

When you stop thinking about your next chapter and don't prepare yourself for the future;

If you don't celebrate your achievements and take good care of yourself, emotionally, physically, mentally and spiritually;

You start dying slowly as a Leader

When you do not have the courage to change your life when you are not satisfied;

If you do not go after your dreams and make them come true;

If you continue to improve candles instead of inventing light;

When you don't allow yourself, occasionally, to take chances, make mistakes and celebrate our imperfection;

If you fail to see that the biggest risk of all is not taking any risk;

Ayalla Reuven- Lelong

PART A:
Michael's Journey
to the Five Lands of Success

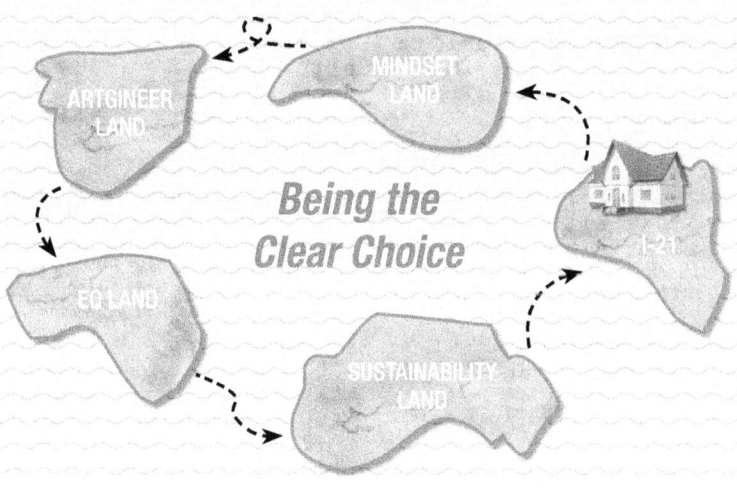

ARTGINEER LAND

MINDSET LAND

Being the
Clear Choice

EQ LAND

SUSTAINABILITY LAND

1-21

1

Setting Out for the Journey: Rowing in White Waters

Michael's Annual Feedback

The seeds of my personal journey as a director at KPMG were sown during an annual feedback session with the head of my department, John, in his spacious office. I remember the conversation and all that followed in great detail. I especially remember stealing a glance off to the sides, checking to see if there was, perhaps, someone else in the room - he simply couldn't be talking about me...

John was an extraordinary leader. Like other partners in our firm, he was highly focused on his tasks; but unlike them, he didn't focus exclusively on the bottom line of the profit and loss statement. He found it important to understand the thinking process of each and every team member. He knew all of us and nurtured a positive atmosphere in the department. He encouraged us to be flexible and creative and to develop personally and professionally. That is why he insisted on conducting an in-depth personal feedback session with each of us.

Formally, all partners were supposed to conduct yearly feedback sessions, but this usually wasn't the case in practice. Even when such sessions did take place, they were often very superficial. It was clear to us that the partners didn't really believe in this tool and saw it as a waste of time, as something that came at the expense of the many daily tasks we were always knee-deep in anyhow.

But John was different. He spoke in terms of "process" and considered himself responsible for leading each and every one of us to realize our full potential. He acted as a kind of mentor. He always spoke about the connection between this process and the vision of our firm. He thought that all leaders and employees should do their best in order to achieve our vision to be the clear choice.

Sounds good, doesn't it? And yet at the time, I would have gladly passed on the opportunity to have a leader like him. All I wanted was a quiet working environment that would allow me to prove myself as an exceptional professional and continue with my annual audit reports.

This year's feedback session, like the two before it, started by focusing on the professional aspects of my work, but it quickly moved on to other areas. It began rather promisingly: John complimented me on my expertise and ability to meet deadlines and noted how impressed he was with my high-level of performance. But these moments of grace were quickly over, as he started detailing the things he thought were still holding me back and how they could be changed.

He began by looking at our firm's values listed on the wall

and asked me if I understood their importance and meaning. I immediately answered that I do. But I also added that, to me, these are no more than a list of beautiful words on the wall. John looked disappointed and started to describe the main findings of Professor Kanter from Harvard Business School about the contribution of values to the business success of the best organizations in the world. He gave me a book with a yellow cover named *SuperCorp*.

"In this book, you will find out what is the role of values in a rapidly changing reality," he said. "You will also learn what makes them so important to the firm and what makes them much more than just beautiful words. Consider it a preparation for your next mentoring session."

What mentoring? I asked myself. Am I supposed to read this book while I have so much work to do?

"And now, regarding your performance as a director, let's be more specific," John continued. "Do you remember what happened two months ago with Tami, our assistant manager? She was forced to stay home with her daughter who came down with a severe case of the flu. When she informed you of the situation, she assured you that she had made sure the team could get along without her. And yet, your reaction was very extreme and lacked empathy. You drove her to tears when you implied that she wasn't really committed to the firm if she chose to neglect her team and compromise the project's deadline."

I wanted to tell him that his conclusion was wrong, that he didn't see my side of the story, but he continued. "Or, for example, during our last global project, when we had to work closely with teams from the UK and Germany, the project manager asked to replace you. Why? Because you didn't get along with the other participants. He claimed that you gave everyone the impression that your opinion was the only one that mattered. When the announcement came, no one really regretted the fact that you were no longer part of the team..."

"Six months ago," he went on, "Roy, our senior partner, introduced the KPMG Story to all of us – our new roadmap to transform our business and unite us all around our shared goals and behavior. According to him, the KPMG Story was essential to our ability to continue to succeed and keep thriving as a firm and to becoming the clear choice. And what was your reaction? Well, you told everyone without even missing one person in the room that this corporate language of big words like vision, purpose and strategy are just bombastic words without any real meaningful outcomes and that you, like many other leaders, are fed up with them.

"You didn't even give it a chance or really try to understand it. Instead, you provided everyone around you with many explanations as to why they should reject it. You kept trying to convince them that the existing state was much better. All along the way, neither the opinions you expressed nor your behavior demonstrated that you were open to any change."

John kept talking in terms of open-mindedness, interpersonal skills, adaptability, creativity and emotional intelligence. I remember telling myself: Here comes the gibberish part, as always, and with it the long-awaited end of our meeting... Just a few more minutes of silence and random nodding on my account – and it would be over.

I was not the only member of our team who had an aversion to terms like vision, purpose, values and "soft skills," with all their touchy-feely connotations. Most of us thought that the introduction of emotional concepts into a "hard skills" firm like ours was a conspiracy led by less talented individuals who couldn't find a more dignified way to make a living.

But this time things didn't go as smoothly as I had expected, and John suddenly turned to me and said: "Listen, Michael, you're proving to be a real challenge for me. I truly think you have exceptional professional skills – but as far as openness, adaptability, creativity and interpersonal skills are concerned, I haven't seen any progress, not even the beginning of a process. With this in mind, I don't think I'll be able to promote you to your next leadership position, at this time. Honestly, it seems that you don't have the necessary leadership skills. I suggest that you schedule a meeting with Martha. Talk to her, and we'll see how to proceed."

This was the point when I started glancing off to the sides to see if there was anyone else in the room. I wasn't used to hearing my name mentioned in relation to words such as "no progress" or "no process." After all, I had graduated with the highest honors. I had always been highly sought-after in my field, and everyone around me saw me as being "successful." John himself said that he always chose me for the most complex technical assignments because it was clear to him that if anyone could overcome the complexity, **I would be the one.**

So where was this whole "unpromotable" label coming from? And why was this whole issue of values, purpose, adaptability and interpersonal skills relevant? After all, I didn't come here to work as an elementary school teacher or a social worker. And yet, it was true that I had recently missed out on two promotion opportunities, despite the fact that everyone knew I was the most suitable candidate for the job, professionally speaking. Come to think of it, I hadn't really progressed as I had wished at my previous job either. For several months now I had been carrying around the feeling that my career hadn't reached the heights it should have… So, what was it that I wasn't getting?

John continued, interrupting my train of thought. "Michael, you are important to me on a personal level," he stated. "That is why I feel the need to stress that as part of your job, it is your responsibility to develop your soft skills, as well as a unique value proposition, in order to become indispensable to the firm. And please bear in mind that what we used to call 'soft skills' are now considered as 'critical skills' which cannot be dismissed any more.

"I know there are heads of departments who hire mediocre professionals because they feel they have no choice. It is relatively easy to find people who know the job, but it is much harder to find professionals who demonstrate mental and practical flexibility, who know how to work effectively in a team and who can deal with the stressful, dynamic and complex reality we face every day.

"You should understand that we can no longer afford mediocre professionals and leaders. Today we understand that in order to be ahead of our competition, we have to hire people who can live our story and achieve our vision. We need people that are highly-qualified in their professional skills, but also in their critical skills, leadership skills and, most importantly, their lifelong learning attitude. Unfortunately, there is nowhere to run or hide nowadays. If you fail to develop these skills, I'm afraid we'll have to pass you over in the next promotion round as well.

"For the future of our firm, we need partners and directors who are able to lead change processes, who work well in a team and who encourage the development of their employees, both professionally and in terms of their emotional intelligence. But most of all, we need leaders who really understand that whatever their role at KPMG is, they need to make a positive impact on society through the work they do; leaders that in their everyday work inspire confidence and empower change and who know what they have to do in-order to be the clear choice of our communities, employees and clients. Leaders who lead by example provide an extraordinary service and offer a winning value proposition to our clients. I have tried to convey this to you so many times in the past, but I feel that my words have fallen on deaf ears."

I left the room feeling confused, as if I had been spoken to in a foreign language I didn't understand. I couldn't comprehend the meaning of these skills, or capabilities, that John spoke of and didn't know how I could go about acquiring them, nor did I know how exactly they were supposed to advance my career. The first thought that crossed my mind was that I'd better quit. After all, any other firm would be glad to have a professional like me as a partner. When I arrived at home, I told my wife Mia about the meeting with John and my thoughts of resigning. At the end of a difficult conversation, she managed to convince me that maybe there was something to what John was saying and that I shouldn't leave my job before all possibilities were exhausted.

On the next morning, the first thing I did was to call Martha, our HR Director, who has a reputation for being sharp and knowing her way around. I remembered the orientation and the advice she gave me when I only started working at the firm, which really helped me get around and understand the organizational balance of power. Martha was welcoming but went straight to the point. "I'd be happy to meet with you," she said, "but take into consideration that this is a long and in-depth process that requires time and dedication, and you must approach it with willingness and open-mindedness. Sadly, as I know too well, many of our leaders are not open to changes of this nature and defiantly dismiss them."

"No problem," I replied, thinking to myself that time would not be an obstacle for me. After all, I do things twice as fast as everyone else. I imagined that in two to three weeks, after one or two meetings with Martha, I would probably be in an entirely different position.

The meeting was scheduled for the next week. I was tense and nervous during the waiting time. I just wanted to get it over with. On the day of the meeting, I went up to Marta's office. Martha welcomed me with a big smile, which slightly eased my concerns. She offered me coffee and asked me to tell her about my expectations. I described my meeting with John, how he told me that he couldn't promote me as long as I failed to develop my critical skills, even though he recognized the fact that I was extremely talented and professional. I explained how confused I was: "It's inconceivable. I feel like someone has changed the rules of the game without bothering to keep me informed."

Martha listened attentively and then said, "Michael, you're not alone. As an HR leader, I can tell you that many professional employees and leaders experience these feelings of frustration and disorientation. It happens in all organizations, regardless of their size and field of activity. The reason is that the rules of the game have really changed. This whole talk about vision, purpose, values and soft skills isn't new; it's been part of the organizational discourse for years. But today, the understanding that these are not just concepts and skills that are "nice to have" has started to sink in. Nowadays, developing such concepts and skills is a key ingredient and critical to being successful, both for individuals and for the organization as a whole."

"So, what does it mean for me?" I asked.

"It means that if, in the past, you could get along thanks to your high professional abilities, which would somehow compensate for your lack of adaptability and leadership skills – and especially for your lack of interpersonal skills – now you don't have this privilege anymore. The reality in which you operate has changed substantially. Today, your success is dependent upon your ability to work in a team, communicate effectively, explore new areas and reinvent yourself – no less than on your professional abilities and performance."

"But you and I both know that our firm is very successful and keeps on growing. Why should we change anything?" I asked.

"Do you remember the central point of Roy's speech during his toast last week?" Martha replied.

The truth was I didn't remember much…

"He said that the fact that the firm is highly successful today doesn't guarantee its ability to continue to be successful in the future. He even quoted from an article by BCG, 'Die Another Day,'¹ which states that the probability that a public company will not survive in the next five years now stands at one in three. The most important part of his speech was when he turned to the firm's partners and directors – you and I included. He said we must all be responsible for our personal development because that is the key that will enable us to reinvent ourselves, to create better products and services, to motivate employees with diverse backgrounds, to be an employer of choice, to differentiate ourselves from the competition and to provide our clients and potential clients with a significant value proposition in order to be their clear choice. He also mentioned the fact that we have an important role in society and therefore we have to make sure that our work quality will be the highest so that we will inspire confidence within the markets and among our clients."

I nodded. I was ashamed to admit that at the time, I thought that Roy was just using over-the-top rhetoric and everything he said seemed meaningless to me.

"Listen, Michael, I've spoken to Roy and John," Martha continued. "They both value you and think you have a good chance of successfully going through this process and becoming a 21st century leader, and a partner in our firm. They both agreed that the firm needs to invest in you and put you through a development process."

For a moment, I panicked.

What did "development process" mean? It sounded as if I was somehow underdeveloped.

Martha noticed my reaction and smiled. "First of all, you can relax. Our firm only allows valuable and high potential leaders to participate in this program. You are about to receive a rare opportunity to embark on a journey that will influence your life in a deep and meaningful way. But you should know that a prerequisite for taking this journey is a true willingness and an honest desire to strengthen those skills and capabilities that leaders need in order to succeed in our changing world – a set of skills whose importance many leaders still don't seem to grasp."

I asked Martha for some time to consider the proposal over the weekend before giving my final answer. I left her office feeling that not only had I not gotten any answers, but my questions and doubts had multiplied.

The thoughts going through my mind during that weekend were jolting. I got the feeling that perhaps I was in the wrong profession, living in the wrong place, at the wrong time. I thought about my father, who worked as a partner in a big accounting firm for most of his life and was never required to undergo what I was going through now. For decades, people had a clear and straightforward job description. But now, just when I came along, the requirements were suddenly changing. Now, in order to be promoted to the senior positions I aspired to, I had to adopt concepts and skills from a world that was entirely foreign to me. The thoughts went on and on in my mind…

Eventually, but not without reservations, I accepted the challenge to embark on the journey, hoping to understand the capabilities that would qualify me to become a successful leader in the 21st century.

The next conversation with Martha was short and concise. She expressed her satisfaction with my decision and handed me Rona's phone number. Rona would be my guide in what she called "The Five Lands Journey."

"I guarantee you that this journey with Rona will be

challenging and exciting, and will open a whole new world for you. Of course, there may be moments when you feel like quitting. But I'm certain that you are not a quitter, and you may rest assured that you won't come back the same person," she said with a wide smile.

Meeting Rona and Changing the Rules of the Game

Shortly after I returned to my office, I called Rona, and we scheduled a meeting. Two days later, when I entered her office, I was surprised to find a beaming woman in her early forties, full of self-esteem. I don't know what I was expecting; I may have pictured a dreary counselor. I immediately started telling her about myself and everything I had talked about with John, sharing my frustrations and asking unfocused questions.

Rona took her time before answering. She didn't take her eyes off me as I spoke, and when I was finally silent, she said pleasantly but authoritatively, "Evidently, we have plenty of work to do…"

Confused, I looked back at her as she continued, "Before you entered my office I went over your impressive résumé. Your professional assessments are also some of the best I've read. But it's apparent that the gap between your professional and soft skills, or critical skills, as we often call them now, is huge. My impression is that sitting in front of me is a guy with low self-awareness, who would prefer no substantial change so that he could go on with his familiar routine; someone who is focused on the mission at hand and incapable of seeing the individuals around him.

"Are you aware that you never even gave me a chance to

introduce myself? You didn't try to lend an ear in order to understand the nature and purpose of this meeting; you didn't try to find out who your audience was in order to adjust your style of communication. In your current state, as a leader, it is evident that you find it hard to create a sense of trust or offer a winning value proposition, abilities that are so important in the world of accountants and advisors. It is also quite clear that you are neither capable of effectively adapting to changes nor can you lead such changes. Still, here you are, telling me how surprised you are that you didn't get promoted."

Ouch! That hurt…

"OK, go on," I replied.

"Michael, from what I see, in the past it was obvious to you, as it was to many of us, that if you went to college and got good grades, the world would be at your feet. However, if you keep on neglecting the skills that you tend to think little of, you will find that the keys to success have passed on to the hands of others."

What keys was she talking about?

Rona turned around and took an orange book off the shelf entitled *A Whole New Mind*, by Daniel Pink.[2]

"To me, this book is very significant. It talks about change that is already taking place, from the knowledge era to an era Pink calls **the conceptual era**. The book describes the circumstances leading to the change. But at this moment, for our purposes, the bottom line is that people like you, the experts of the information age, are already unable to supply all the goods. Leaders who wish to succeed in a reality that is rapidly changing before our eyes must adopt a wider approach, integrating qualities that were discarded in the past. They will have to be more creative and innovative, and these concepts will have to encompass broader meanings than in the past. Naturally, professional skills and technical know-how will still remain central in any new era, but professionals and leaders will also be in need of other critical skills."

"The future belongs to those who are able to merge different fields, who are open to learning in all aspects of their profession and who can instill a sense of purpose in everyday processes and motivate people in a complex reality. Those who can reinvent themselves will be able to offer a compelling value proposition that truly resonates with the firm and its clients. Individuals who master these skills will be the ones that determine the mindset of modern life. And you, Michael, definitely want to be there."

I must admit that I didn't quite understand what the hell she was talking about, or what all this had to do with my feedback conversation with John or with my success. Nonetheless, I made every effort to hide my feelings. Besides, the thought of the promises I had made to Mia and to Martha motivated me, and I quickly replied, "OK, I'm ready. When are we going?"

Rona smiled. "Wait a minute. Before we go, we must prepare for the journey and understand what caused the rules of the game to change. Any significant process of change begins for certain reasons."

"I'm listening."

"In order to understand today's reality, we must return to the mid-18th century, to the beginning of the industrial revolution. Human society made the shift from manual to industrial production and discovered the power of machines and mass production. This revolution initiated significant social and economic changes. At first, the pace of the changes could be measured in terms of 'half-a-century' or decades. Since then, the pace of change has continuously increased as the result of accelerated industrial, technological and economic development.

"Technology has changed the face of modern society and economy. Industrial production has brought about great wealth in terms of higher quality and lower prices of products, but has also led to fierce competition. In recent years, much of the manufacturing has been relocated to East Asia due to the availability of cheaper manpower, further increasing the competition and operational complexity.

"As the East Asian economies strengthen and the reach of the Internet expands, competition continues to escalate. It is now commonly expected that some of the knowledge-intensive professions will also relocate to East Asia, just as did the manufacturing. Various professional services such as accounting, law, financial management and even high-tech development, are already available as offshore and outsourcing services from India or China, at a quality that is not inferior to that of their Western counterparts and at a significantly lower cost."

"So, why is this new?" I asked. "It's widely known that nowadays everyone is continuously competing with everyone for everything, everywhere."

"First, remember that since the industrial revolution, the world has seen several cycles of change," Rona answered. "Eventually, accompanied by many social revolutions, these changes brought about better lives for many people in the western world and created a wealthy middle class that enjoys stable growth and even better prospects for their children. However, there are many warning signs that this time, it's going to be different.

"What is new today is that this dynamic reality has crossed a threshold – it is so intense, broad and profound that it truly is a game changer. That is to say, it brings about changes in the rules of the game and, accordingly – changes in the skills required for success.

"Today, there is a consensus that in the next few decades of the 21st century, the economy will undergo a change of a kind that we have not witnessed in the past two hundred years.

"This situation can be compared to the reality of **white water rafting**. The question is no longer whether or not we will fall, but rather when it will happen. Then, when we are in the water, the question is whether we can board the raft once again. Michael, you must understand that the odds are not in our favor."

"Not in our favor in what respect?" I asked…

"Current studies show that only 30% of organizations and managers will be able to 'board the raft again' successfully, to continue with this metaphor. And even then, they will have to deal with a different reality, meaning that the raft will already be in a different place. And if we're already speaking of the organizational world in terms of survival, it's worth mentioning that Charles Darwin, the 'father' of the theory of evolution, didn't actually claim that the strongest, fastest or even smartest are the fittest to survive, but rather those who are best capable of adapting to their environment, especially in a changing one.

"One key factor for adaptation and survival is cooperation. That is why in a changing environment like the one we are currently experiencing, each organization must see to it that the best people work together, in cooperation, guided by a common purpose and motivated by a strong value system – I'm talking about the KPMG Story, in our case.

"But this alone is not enough. Securing the continuity of success demands that organizations allocate their resources wisely between present requirements and future needs. They must be able to perform their ongoing activities in order to successfully meet the current challenges, while at the same time progressively adapting these very same activities to changes and anticipated changes... Studies show that very few can do both simultaneously."

"And what is it that enables such simultaneous performance?" I wondered.

"Organizations need leaders capable of connecting with people, viewing challenging situations in a positive light and assuming responsibility for all organizational and personal processes. This is why our abilities to adapt to changes, leave our comfort zone, develop and grow are of crucial importance to our ongoing success, on both the personal and the organizational level.

"But before you leave your own comfort zone and embark on this journey, let's go over the factors that change the rules of the game and create the white waters I was talking about."

The Factors that Change the Rules of the Game

"Look," Rona continued, "I'm not an expert in economics and business management, but one thing is clear to me and to everyone else: the reality we once knew is changing dramatically, and there are many factors inducing this change."

"I would like to focus on seven factors that came up during in-depth interviews conducted by Steve Tappin with about 150 senior executives. Tappin is a counselor and confidant of top-notch senior executives from global organizations. He included these interviews in a book called *The Secrets of CEOs*[3], which he wrote together with economic journalist Andrew Cave. The two also followed it up with a sequel they wrote after conducting an additional round of interviews with 200 senior executives."[4]

She handed me a tablet and said, "Take this – it will guide us on our journey. On the screen you can see the result of those interviews – the list of the top seven game changers. These are the major factors that are changing the rules of the

The Rules of the Game are Changing

- Economic Crises
- Globalization
- Sustainability
- Technology
- Regulation
- Generation Y
- Competition for every Customer

game and creating the reality of white water rafting. As you will see, there is a strong connection between the different factors."

1. Economic Crises

"The first factor mentioned is **economic crises**. In the past, an economic crisis would occur about every 20 or 30 years. Nowadays, one crisis follows another. Every day I open the financial section of the newspaper and panic. Nobel Prize laureates in economics speak of a lost decade in financial terms. In light of the massive protests that have been taking place and the situation in the markets in Europe and the United States, it is obvious that there aren't many reasons to be optimistic."

"I agree with you," I answered. "In terms of uncertainty and the frequency of economic crises and recoveries, it feels like we are actually rafting in white waters."

"Yes. And please consider the fact that the many global changes taking place, which are already influencing us, may affect our daily work even further. Senior executives struggle to manage in the best possible way, juggling between risks and opportunities. If in the past, they waited for better conditions in order to act and take new initiatives, most organizations now realize that they must learn to act under constant uncertainty in order to succeed. Sure, uncertainty has always existed, but today it also affects organizations and business areas which were once immune to it."

"OK, I know about globalization, but what global changes are you talking about?"

2. Globalization

"Your question brings us to the second factor, **globalization**. It is well known that the world has become a small village. Globalization influences organizations and is a major element leading to the deepening and expansion of competition. That is why it is an important game changer. In the past, globalization consisted of getting a foothold – business organizations, mostly western ones, opened branches in other countries and acted as if these were just local replicas of the original headquarters. Today, it's impossible to act this way. Many enterprises failed because they couldn't understand local customers, local needs and the different management cultures in these emerging new markets. Those who tried to impose prices, products or western business models didn't realize their expectations most of the time.

"However, the organizations that did well were usually those who successfully decoded the local culture and needs: what the customers want, how to provide it to them, how to solve their problems and how to handle the various locally specific challenges. These organizations were also wise enough to define long-term business objectives and a global strategy based on local human infrastructures – building a chain of talented local executives and employees.

"In today's reality, the successful organizations are those that adopt a global mindset, realizing that their role is not only to bring their own skills to the developing countries but also to merge, understand and share. These are the organizations that can internalize and incorporate the values of the new place to the same extent as the values they bring with them as a foreign culture. Think about this aspect of integrating an existing business into a foreign culture – the aspiration for mutuality. You'll realize that the importance of skills such as empathy, flexibility and reality testing cannot be underestimated for executives in these places."

"And still," I said, "If we look at the last events in the world, we can see that globalization has taken some hard blows, like the Brexit. As you probably know, Rona, very soon the UK will probably leave the European Union. Talking about the Brexit and the white-water rapids, many of our clients are confused and even panic. They need our help in navigating through this storm. They will need us to help them understand how Brexit is going to influence their EU workers, businesses' supply chains and cash flows."

"Michael, you are very right, we see new events all over the word that are very dramatic. As I see it, there may be some slowdown of globalization, but it is hard to imagine a real reversal in the modern connected world. It will be very interesting to see to what direction we are headed."

"Well, we will see. However, going back to what you said earlier about empathy, with all due respect to empathy," I continued, "you and I both know that eventually our success is measured by the stockholders according to the quarterly results. Eventually, any long-term investment decreases short-term profits."

3. Sustainability

"You should note that this paradigm has shifted, Michael. And this is where the third factor comes into play – **sustainability**, but more specifically – the viability of the business, its ability to persist and maintain at least the same level of success over time.

"What's new is that the bottom line is no longer determined merely by our profit and loss statement, and the short-term bottom line is no longer how organizational results are presented to stockholders.

"Across professional fields, even in the business world, organizations are realizing that not only their expenses and profitability play a part in their success, but also their image. They now understand that their image has a lot of impact, especially in the long run. The definition of success has expanded to include the positive influence on society at large. Executives in the 21st century must take into account this broader definition of success and build their organizational strategy accordingly. They must incorporate it into their decision-making, measurement and evaluation processes, and they must explain it clearly to their shareholders, whether they be financial bodies, governmental institutions or the public."

"Basically, what happened is that the sustainability of the business has become tightly linked to its contribution to the overall viability of the communities, economies and environments in which it operates."

Of all the things I had heard so far, this was the weirdest. "Now listen here, Rona. With all due respect to the environment and the community, today's businesses suffer from fierce competition. While they struggle to lower their expenses, you're talking about more spending. Eventually, no one will remember your generosity when your business collapses. After all, we do pay state taxes, property taxes and social security, and it's the state's job to help others, isn't it?"

"Michael, our entire society is changing and people are empowered like never before. The current situation makes it impossible to ignore the issue of sustainability. In this respect, I believe we have better years ahead of us – when organizations won't be all about profits and will contribute to society as well. I know that PepsiCo, Cisco and IBM are already there. A highly esteemed Harvard professor, Rosabeth Moss Kanter, spearheads this type of process in leading global organizations. She published an excellent book in which she describes the contribution of these organizations to society.[5] She argues that organizations that are wise enough to work this way will continue to grow and profit."

"So you argue that processes foreseen by actuaries of risk, economists and others should make us completely change concepts which have evolved and proven themselves for more than a century? Where were these wise men before the last crisis? I believe that a significant part of what they're saying is a reflection of the pressure resulting from a decade of recession. But other than forecasts, do you have any examples of evident changes?"

4. Technology

"Of course, and this leads me to one of the central factors in the creation of white waters: **technology**. The Internet is constantly reinventing itself. Each time it takes over another aspect of our lives, whether related to work or leisure. Although I will focus on the Internet and mostly on what is called Web 3.0, you should remember that, as we speak, my knowledge of recent technological trends may already be out-of-date.

"The first Internet wave was based on static sites intended

only for public image and web presence, sites that merely promote the business but do not really offer anything for sale. The business community was surprised by the rise of global sales sites such as Amazon, which also led to changes in consumption habits and to new business models.

"The second wave, Web 2.0, turned surfers into content producers. The rise of social networks completely changed business models in the sectors of media, entertainment and advertising. This wave also permanently changed commerce, the banking system, etc.

"The third wave, Web 3.0, is mostly based on the wide availability of technologies that are the backbone of what is now called "the cloud" – fast communication infrastructures, especially wireless, and the establishment of huge server farms, storing vast amounts of data and providing modular and flexible computing systems.

"Earlier, I mentioned the migration of services to rising economy countries. It is mainly the result of the availability of new information technologies: virtualization technologies that enable you to work with a person at the other end of the world as if he were in the next room. But that's just the tip of the iceberg…

"Consumers now enjoy a huge variety of devices and interfaces, mobile touchscreen devices which offer a total and even addictive experience. Overall, this is a revolution that changed not only the way we live and communicate, but also business models, human resources requirements, and what is required of us, the executives."

"Often, the Internet is referred to as a 'disruptive technology,' because every wave of change disrupts business models and can topple giants who weren't prepared for it. Meanwhile, small unknown companies such as Amazon, Google and Facebook became large corporations. As consumers began flowing to the e-commerce sites, the media channels also migrated to the Internet. Social networks feasted on the remains of people's attention and free time, taking over what used to be the business of the old entertainment and marketing channels.

"As a business, if you don't join the new virtual worlds, you are left behind, unknown and unheard of. You just don't exist anymore. As an individual, whether you are an executive or not, if you desire to progress professionally you must understand how these new technologies affect your profession. Otherwise, you will belong to the past and linger there.

"You are surely unaware of this, but with the emergence of the Internet, most CEOs dismissed it, thinking that it was something for geeks, with no real business value. Can you imagine?

"Today the situation is different; nobody can dismiss the technological changes and their consequences. I recently talked to a senior executive who heads the IT department at one of the major banks. I realized that the lack of knowledge as to what the future holds, from a technological standpoint, is driving everyone off balance. Compared to the previous waves, the third Internet wave is the least understood, even by CEOs. Even if most of them are aware of the great impact of technology on the organizations they lead, about 60% of them admit that they don't have a sufficient understanding of technology and its impact.

"Everyone understands now that effectively handling

the third Internet wave is the biggest challenge of the next few decades. The popular perception is that these new technologies will create a larger revolution and will change business models in a way that will make Web 2.0 look like child's play."

"Last month," Rona continued, "I read the '*2016 Global CEO Outlook*' of KPMG with the title '*Now or Never.*' In this survey, a significant majority of CEOs recognize the important need to foster a culture of innovation, respond quickly to technological opportunities and invest in new processes. But most CEOs recognize that they are now handling issues they have never grappled with before. More important, the majority of CEOs believe that technological change will be one of the biggest factors impacting growth over the next three years, second only to economic factors – the topic we started our conversation with."

"So now," I said, "I fully understand that technological progress requires adaptation and adjustment. But this change is eventually for the best! Last week, for example, I read a very interesting article about the 4th industrial revolution, which is going to change our lives completely. Experts say that the transformation will be unlike anything humankind has experienced before. There are great opportunities here, and I personally find it very exciting. So, what's the problem?"

"There is no problem *per se*," she replied. "But this definitely does require adaptation, flexibility and the ability to make optimal use of the new technologies to manage your work. But many individuals and organizations will find it difficult to cope with this type of change, as will many accountants, whether tech-savvy or not. Don't take it personally..." The last comment was accompanied with a smile and a joking expression. She did have a sense of humor...

"To be more specific, the accounting profession itself faces a major shift as many companies invest in software systems that will transform the auditing process into an automated, low-cost commodity. The future of audit is very clear to most of us. Artificial Intelligence based on 'big data' will perform many of the tasks that today's accountants still perform. As a result, revenues will flow away from the firms, which will have to reduce costs by keeping only those accountants who have a winning value proposition and a more up-to-date set of skills.

"One thing is sure, as Mr. John Veihmeyer the Chairman of KPMG International stated[6] – '*It reminds us all at KPMG that we need to continue to match this pace of change and constantly apply innovative approaches to meet our clients' evolving needs, whether they seek advice for targeted change programs or end-to-end support for enterprise-wide transformation.*'"

5. Regulation

"And this brings us to the fifth factor that is changing the rules of the game – **regulation**.

"Regardless of the organization I'm lecturing at – whenever I meet executives and talk about their challenges, I know that the regulator is breathing down their necks. No matter the sector they operate in, regulation is increasingly prevalent, restricting the organizations and their ability to operate freely. Executives know they must meet all the regulatory terms and develop a rigorous organizational discipline to comply with the requirements.

"One could say that the regulatory changes we are seeing are the mirror image of the quantity and complexity of the changes taking place in society, in the economy and with regard to technology. They are also the result of previous failures, which led to crises and social protests. But either way, these regulatory changes are forcing organizations to think differently – to think not only about their immediate short-term profit but also about the long term and in wider circles."

"OK," I said. "It reminds me that I heard John quoting Jane McCormick, the Global Head of Tax at KPMG, saying that[7] *'Regulatory compliance, if not approached properly, can hamper transformation and growth.'* She also said that CEOs are fully aware of its importance and that many of them *'see regulatory risk as the second most important risk, after cyber risk.'*

"So, how do we deal with all these changes in practice?" I asked. "Let me guess: the answer has to do with human resources?"

"Well, I am not an expert in regulation and its implementation," Rona replied. "But I can firmly state that as part of the human resources of an organization, a leader can no longer operate as a 'lone wolf' and must also learn to function as a link in the chain – as part of a team, department, organization, and community. I can assure you that there was no other period in organizational history in which the set of skills of an organization's leaders was as important to the organization's success as it is in today's complex reality."

6. Generation Y

"But what is also very interesting and important to note with regard to human resources is that we have witnessed significant changes with the entrance of **Generation Y** into the workforce, another factor contributing to the white waters."

"Yes, I am quite familiar with this generation," I said, immediately evoking my personal experience. "I'm surrounded by them at work. It's those energetic, young and vibrant employees who always know everything and expect everything to come quickly – promotions, professional development, feedback, higher salaries…, and the list goes on…"

"They also live with their parents, drive their parents' cars and spend their parents' money," I joked. "It's a generation of people that have just started to learn something and already want to move on to the next challenge. From what I've seen, the biggest problem with this generation is that their self-esteem is inversely proportionate to their level of experience."

"There is no doubt that this generation is different from the previous ones, the Baby Boomers and Generation X," Rona smiled. "This generation is also proving to be a challenge to managers and senior management in unprecedented levels. But more and more leaders and managements now understand that their ability to compete depends mainly on the quality of their employees: good employees mean good business performance and vice versa…

"In the past, many leaders stated that 'our people are our greatest asset,' but this was not really reflected in any way in the workplace. In today's reality, actualizing this conception is critical to the growth of any organization."

"There!" I rejoiced. "You said it yourself! The best should be kept and rewarded. So we are back to the good old professional skills: professionals who are wizards in their area of expertise, brilliant and incisive."

"Well, no, Michael. I am definitely not talking only about professional skills. Despite everything you said about Generation Y, and many leaders think like you, this is the generation that will dominate the marketplace. By all accounts, it's a very challenging generation. It's the first generation that grew up under what we call 'conscious parenting': their parents talked to them and listened to them. They told them things like 'If you dislike something, you don't have to do it' or 'It's important to us that you're happy and can fulfill yourself,' and of course, 'You are very talented and you can be anything you want to be.' So, indeed, when they come to the workplace, this generation feels very worthy, and they do want to have it all: a high salary, a quick promotion, work-life balance, an executive talk after a week at the job, close monitoring, and more…"

"But do not be mistaken, Michael. This generation will make the world a better place for all of us. And you know why? Because it's the first time in organizational history that organizations are changing their strategies in order to preserve the best employees. Most organizations now understand that all they really have is their people. They adopt an '*Employer of Choice*' strategy, which asks what the organization can do to be the first choice for the best employees and preserve them over time, and promote those who are most fit for leadership and management positions."

"And your job is to find the best ones," I added.

"It is indeed," Rona replied. "And it's worth noting that for the first time in history, and mainly because the retirement age has been delayed, four different generations now find themselves working together. These are generations with different work ethics, different values, and one could even say they speak different languages... Sometimes it seems to me that they're from entirely different planets! The generation gap will influence every process in the organization: recruitment, promotion, benefits, career paths, and the business side of things, of course. And in that context, to quote the 2016 CEOs Outlook again: '*99 percent of CEOs report taking action to develop existing or future talent.*'

"It is clear that in a reality like this, an organization's Human Resources Department plays a critical role. An advanced HR department that is aligned with the organizational strategy and provides significant added value will undoubtedly spur the growth of any successful organization.

"As for Generation Y, what's interesting is that despite everything that's said about them, Millennials know how to provide excellent services to their customers. But we also have to remember that many of the customers themselves are from Generation Y, and as such, they also differ from previous generations of customers. It is generally advisable to make sure that they come out satisfied, because they have the ability to voice their criticism and spread their dissatisfaction in ways that could reach hundreds of thousands of people in just a short time.

7. Competition for Every Customer

"Which leads me to the last factor creating the white waters, and definitely not the least important one – **fierce competition for every customer**, whether an existing customer or a potential one. We are talking about the top concern of almost all CEOs.

"Today's clients are very picky: they demand higher quality services and products for half the price. On the other hand, many of these services and products have become commodities, which most companies can provide at a fairly similar level of quality, speed and price.

"In such a situation, all types of customers and clients, even CEOs and CFOs, are aware of the many choices they have. As a result, business organizations feel that they have to be more creative, to keep on reinventing themselves, in order to offer an attractive and unique value proposition. In these circumstances, and especially in our firm, the ability of leaders and employees to connect and create a relationship based on trust is critical. I'm talking about being able to become a 'trusted advisor' to one's strategic client and not just a service vendor. You know, firms like ours can differentiate themselves in many ways. But in all aspects of communication with clients, the emotional intelligence of those who are in direct contact with the clients play a vital role."

The Consequences of the Change

"OK, I think I understand. But if this is the reality, what does it mean for management in general and for me as a future leader?" I asked.

"As a director, it is important that you understand that ongoing change will continue to be a defining characteristic of the business and organizational environment. To succeed in such an environment, leaders must be open-minded and know how to initiate and lead change. What was true yesterday is no longer true today, and will definitely not be true tomorrow. Leaders must know how to undergo change themselves – how to 'stay on the raft' over time – but also how to motivate and lead their teams in times of constant change.

"Leading teams has become a complicated and dynamic process, far more than it has ever been before. If the carrot and stick approach used to be effective, today much more is necessary. In the past, employees were afraid of their managers and felt compelled to obey them. But nowadays, their motivation requires much more. Leaders have to use a different style of leadership. They must bring their teams closer to them using their personality as leaders. Daniel Pink stresses[8] that executives must have high-level leadership skills and give their employees a sense of autonomy, enabling them to become experts while providing them with meaning in the work environment."

"These are all things that we will discuss during our journey. I have chosen a track for us that will allow us to experience and delve deeper into all the issues we have discussed thus far."

"I'm intrigued…"

"Very well… And if so, I would like to share some more insights with you and elaborate a little bit more on some of the white water generators that we've just introduced.

"The first and most significant one is that in the not-so-distant future, there will be a heavy shortage of talented executives and employees, capable of managing and working in such a complex world of continuous and accelerating changes. Undoubtedly, in light of this uncertainty, this complex world requires broader skills and abilities from leaders. Most people find it hard to change, so they cling to the mental maps that led them to success so far. Recently, the Center for Creative

Leadership[9] conducted an interesting study. The study concluded that most organizations wouldn't appoint about 40% of their managers if they had to make the decision again."

This is a harsh and rather troubling finding, I thought to myself.

"I can see the wheels turning in your head. Listen, I take part in quite a few processes in leading organizations here. I sit in meetings where executives try to decide who to promote and I see how hard it is to find suitable candidates. For instance, Nathan has superb professional abilities, but he is unable to manage even a single employee; Emma has excellent leadership skills, but she's not professional enough; Dana has a high level of professional skills and her employees love her, but she is incapable of reaching the senior managements of her clients. I have no doubt that in today's complex world, leaders need a far broader set of skills and capabilities in order to succeed.

"And one more thing. Try to understand that the most important skills for success will be the critical skills, or emotional intelligence. You probably know that most higher education institutes only accept candidates with strong cognitive skills. This selection method greatly minimizes the differentiation between professionals, leaving mostly attributes and abilities that derive from their soft skills, or critical skills, as we often call them now.

"There are many people with a bachelor's, master's, or a doctoral degree. Generation Y loves to study. The economic situation drives them to spend more time in school and get one more degree, in order to improve their chances of being hired for one of the best positions.

"So what is unique about those who succeed in becoming

leaders? Obviously, there are leaders whose exceptional abilities stand out, like in every field. But it turns out that what differentiates between them is their emotional intelligence. When I talk to executives about the concept of ideal leaders, they wholly admit that what sets them apart are soft skills or components of emotional intelligence, even if they don't use this specific terminology.

"Think about your own work environment, and you'll notice that the ones who succeed are those with strong skills in this field. These are the passionate, flexible, adaptable and determined leaders, who lead and initiate changes, who work well in a team, who have a high sense of social responsibility and who are sought after by clients and other firms alike."

"I have to admit that I've never given this any thought," I professed.

"One thing that I can say with certainty," Rona said in a tone of summary, "is that if emotional intelligence was important for success in the 20th century, it is absolutely critical for success in the 21st century."

"There is another aspect making emotional intelligence so important to the organization. Employees and executives will require extremely high emotional intelligence in order to retain existing clients and recruit new ones. Moreover, even the strongest and well-positioned organizations will need people who possess the ability to build significant relationships with their clients – based on high levels of trust and providing a real value proposition. Only when most of their executives have such abilities can the management claim to be on the right path…

"Emotional intelligence is also very important in your profession from another perspective. Knowledge-expert employees will indeed continue to control the market, and lifelong learning will be a business requirement. Let me explain this point through a very interesting finding I read about several years ago in the *Harvard Business Review*, which made me think deeply about the subject. Twenty-five years ago, when a student graduated and joined the workforce, how much of the knowledge he acquired during his studies do you think he made use of?"

"Most of it?" I guessed.

"Correct, the answer is about 75%. The rest of the knowledge was gradually acquired from professional guidebooks and individuals within the organization. After a certain amount of time, the knowledge he had acquired made him a professional. Dedication and experience made him an expert.

"Today, things are dramatically different: a typical graduate on his first job will use about 10% of the knowledge he acquired during his studies. This knowledge is not necessarily the most essential or the most required for success on the job. Actually, his studies provided him with a mostly theoretical base of knowledge for his profession. From this point, through various positions he will hold, begins the acquisition of practical knowledge and experience in the real world.

"In an era of continuous innovation, the subject matter is not updated quickly enough, and a professional will have to acquire most of the required knowledge throughout his career. This need will probably never cease; both he and his more senior colleagues will have to continue to gain new knowledge and adapt to new technologies and to a changing reality. As a result, continuous lifelong learning will be a business requirement and a precondition for ongoing success. The expert of today cannot lie back, relax and believe that he's seen it all and knows it all."

"But this isn't something new," I protested. "For us who operate in the financial and regulatory worlds, this has always been the case."

"You are right Michael. Learning and keeping updated has always been a part of your profession. But this process has become more challenging than ever. What is different now is the amount and the pace of the changes, the rate at which new technologies, events and regulations affect the accounting world.

"And more importantly, from my experience, I know that only those who truly love what they do are capable of substantial learning. If you don't love what you do, any learning process, whether individually or in a group, will be an unwelcome task, something you will try to avoid.

"The reality in the 21st century is very challenging, so it's important that you know that the professionals and leaders who will succeed in the 21st century will be those who integrate high professional abilities, high emotional intelligence and strong business skills. They are those who understand their business and the business of their clients, who take responsibility for their personal development and the development of their colleagues. They are also those who are enthusiastic about their work over time, determined, flexible and proactive."

"So how do we actually get there?"

"There is no doubt that in your case, we'll have to go through all the five lands mentioned by Martha and get to know them closely. Like every journey, you will be able to obtain exciting and meaningful experiences from each place. Like every journey, this one will also introduce you to new sights, cultures and people. And like every journey, you will have to cope with new experiences in terms of uncertainty, meeting challenges and correctly allocating your resources.

"But eventually, the emphasis in this journey is on the internal, mental and emotional change that you will have to undergo. Do not panic... I'm not talking about a spiritual experience. I'm talking about acquiring skills – most of which are measurable, you'll be surprised to learn. These skills will enable you to act from a better place, from a position of leadership, power and awareness.

"This journey will actually enable you, and many other leaders in KPMG, to live our story – the KPMG Story – to the fullest; increase the pride and confidence of our people, deepen connections with our clients, strengthen public trust in our profession and in business as a whole, and eventually, become the clear choice. Some senior partners have told me that this journey is the only way to make sure that we all have the mindset, skills and competencies that are necessary to live our story and inspire our leaders and employees.

"Remember Michael, in order to live the KPMG Story, and share it all around the world, we need the full commitment and engagement of our partners and directors."

"So, when and where are we going?" I asked, surprised by the intensity of my enthusiasm.

"We're leaving early tomorrow morning. I know you don't have much time to pack, but we don't need much for such a journey. What we need most is an open mind. I'll meet you two hours before boarding; I have a few important messages for you before you set off."

That night, before leaving, I gave up on trying to sleep. As I packed a small suitcase, I was unable to part with the skepticism that accompanied me in spite of my great excitement and curiosity. I tried to rearrange my thoughts and cope with the fears that arose, hoping that this journey would not become a worthless experience that would hinder me in one of my most significant accounts.

When I met Rona at the coffee counter at the airport, she appeared fresh, though slightly pensive. "Hello Michael," she said and smiled her wide smile, "I'm happy to see you. I know it wasn't easy for you to take the first step and go on this journey. Let's get a table and see what's happening here before we board the plane."

Did we come to look at people? – I thought to myself. Is this why she asked me to come early to the airport?

"I know it sounds trivial, Michael, but one of the most important things to remember is that each one of us is unique – a world in itself. Do you see the couple seated next to us and hardly talking? Did you notice the father explaining to his daughter why she can't have that expensive doll? Look at the woman sitting and smoking one cigarette after another and the businessman who can't stop talking on his cell phone and working on his computer. Do you see that beautiful cashier that everyone is checking out? Each of them has their own mental map, or if you wish, their own thinking pattern or mindset. Our actions, our decisions and our considerations, the extent of the effort we make and our faith in ourselves – these are all the consequences of mindsets."

"And what does it all have to do with our purpose, vision and leadership?" I asked.

"As a future leader, in order to be able to become the clear choice, it is important for you to become acquainted with two major types of thinking patterns: the fixed mindset and the growth mindset[10]. Understanding these two thinking patterns and telling them apart is one of the most important lessons, without which it is impossible to move on. Soon we will see how these concepts influence our daily lives–both our organizational and our personal lives. You don't have children yet, but later on you will find out that your understanding of these two concepts will significantly influence your children and their lives."

At this point, I felt once again that perhaps I had made a mistake by setting out on this journey. What was she talking about? What did my promotion at work have to do with the children I didn't have yet? As I tried to quiet down the critical voice inside me, I heard the call: "Passengers on Flight 311 to Mindset Land, please report to gate No. 4."

"But Rona!" I yelled, trying to make myself heard over the loud noise that burst from the jet engines before takeoff, "At the end of the journey, how will I know if I've succeeded?"

Rona smiled and replied "You will know it once you can't keep all the insights you have acquired to yourself; when you have a tremendous urge to share them with the rest of the world; when you come back to work and strive for all your nearest and dearest to internalize these insights; when you don't understand how it is possible to think or act otherwise. Then you'll know you have successfully completed the journey and have become a leader fit for the 21st century."

The Leader as one who is both an engineer and an artist: critical and strategic thinker, analytical and methodological; yet also intuitive, visionary, creative, relationship driven and passionate about his area of expertise, clients and employees.

Artgineer Land

Becoming the

EQ Land

Sustainability Land

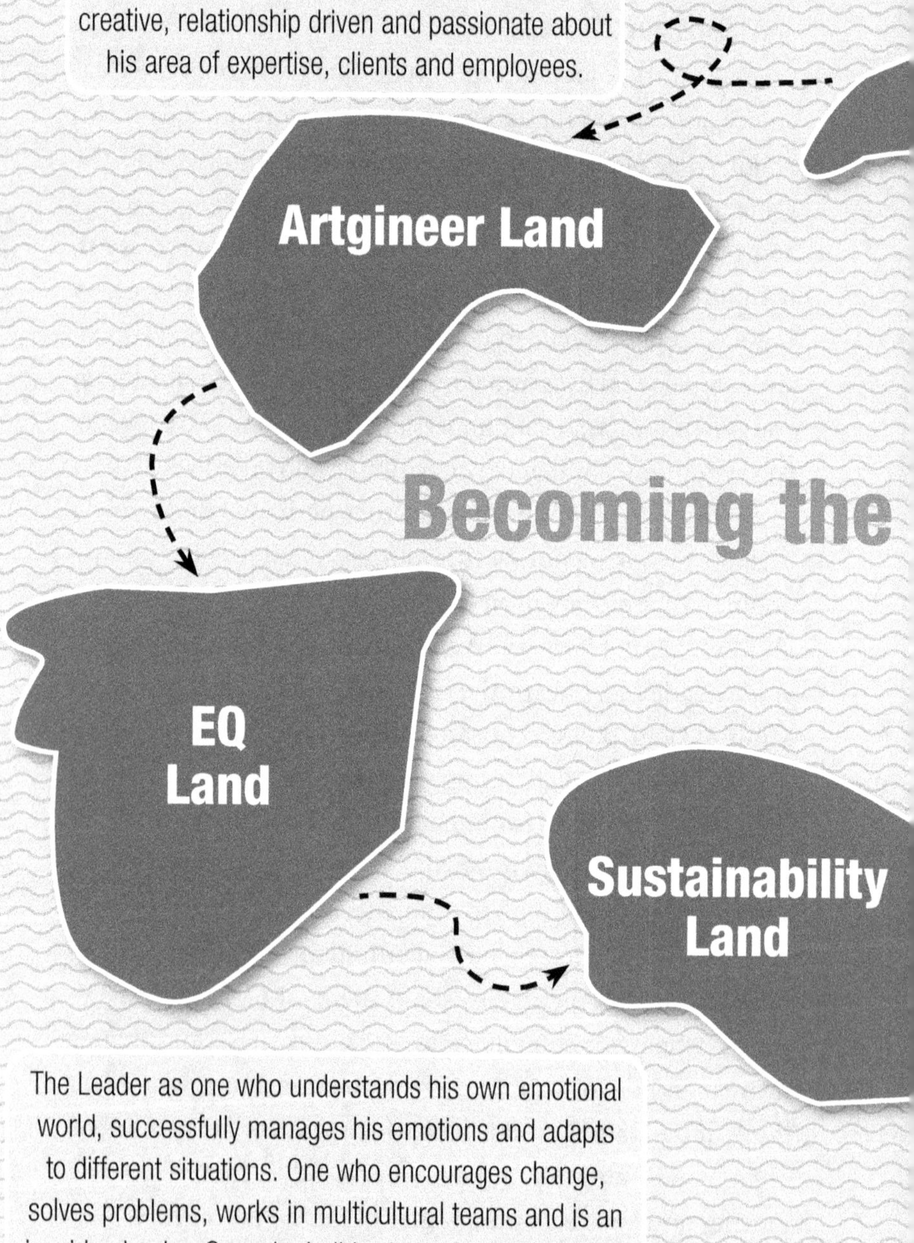

The Leader as one who understands his own emotional world, successfully manages his emotions and adapts to different situations. One who encourages change, solves problems, works in multicultural teams and is an inspiring leader. One who builds close relationships with his clients and becomes their Trusted Advisor.

The Leader as one who is a lifelong learner in 5 areas: professional, emotional, technological, business and leadership

Mindset Land

Clear Choice

I-21

The Leader as one who re-invents himself and develops a compelling and winning value proposition (both for himself and for his team).

The Leader as one who can succeed over time in the gushing white waters – who finds a deep purpose in his work, takes ownership over his career, connects with sponsors and mentors in order to learn and develop, positively frames a challenging reality (both for himself and his team) and understands that one has to maintain his own wellbeing.

2

Mindset Land

The destination Rona chose to begin with was called Mindset Land. She explained that the term mindset means a thinking pattern.

We arrived early in the morning. As the pilot descended for landing, Rona drew my attention to a long river, stretching from the horizon to the ocean. On one of the river's banks was a colorful and upbeat urban area, while on the other bank there were straight lines of dreary, gray buildings. Rona told me these were the two banks of the capital city of Mindset Land. I was hoping to start our tour from the colorful side of the city, which seemed much more interesting and appealing.

It was a soft landing. From the airport, we drove to town and started sightseeing. We walked a lot and talked little. I guess Rona wanted me to experience the place on my own and have an unbiased impression of it.

Well, my first impression of the place, as I saw it from the plane's window, turned out to be true. The urban scene on the west side of the city, where we started our tour, was indeed colorful, lively and exciting. Impressive buildings were everywhere, and the most prominent thing was the wide diversity of styles. We saw skyscrapers alongside ornate cathedrals, lively piazzas with sculptures and fountains and many entertainment centers: art galleries, theaters and cinemas. Advertising posters for dozens of shows were posted, and everywhere we looked there were street shows and open-air concerts. The many museums were surrounded by gardens and parks. We saw a variety of stores and small boutiques that were adjacent to large shopping malls. The business sector made it clear that this city was a large commercial and economic center. On the modern buildings, we saw signs with the logos of Banks, financial companies and technology companies such as Google, Microsoft, Cisco and Facebook. In the broad spaces between the buildings, we saw people rushing to work with cups of coffee in their hands. But here, unlike other commercial cities I had visited around the world, I saw smiling people who seemed pleased and relaxed. It clearly appeared that they were enthusiastic and even passionate about their activities.

The interesting thing was that in each piazza, regardless of its size, was a colorful and creatively designed monument paying homage to men and women who "made it," decorated with portraits and descriptions of their lives and accomplishments. These commentaries revealed the concepts that were the foundation of their achievements, the challenges they faced and praise for their determination and efforts. These monuments impressed me and added a facet of intimacy to the lively place. Even after three hours of touring, I still wanted to spend more time in this city.

When we reached the main street, referred to by the locals as "Restaurant Street," we discovered a beautiful mall, paved with stone. It had all kinds of restaurants – Italian, Chinese, Japanese, Cuban, Portuguese and many others. Astounded by the abundance and the sense of unlimited possibilities, I suggested that we have lunch.

We finally chose a local tapas bar, sat in its well-groomed yard as the waiter took our order. I was surprised that immediately afterward, a kind and hearty man carrying a tray with plates of food approached us. He introduced himself as Mario, the owner. Mario was interested to find out where we came from and who told us about his restaurant. After a while, I expressed my surprise that such a successful restaurant owner could find the time to talk to his customers at such a busy time of day. He laughed and said that his curiosity and desire to learn from new people were his guidelines, the same guidelines that served all the other citizens on this side of the river.

"The people on this side of the river are curious people. We are constantly learning new things, growing and evolving," he said, smiling.

When he saw my confused look, he further explained, "Unlike our neighbors on the other side of the river, we were nurtured by the understanding that regardless of our starting point, the most important thing in life is to continuously learn and develop. We believe that personal skills develop and intensify throughout life."

He went on to tell us that their lives were guided by the concept that the brain itself is a flexible and dynamic organ, capable of changing and growing through learning and practice.

"Did you just say that the brain changes?" I wondered skeptically, "In what sense? After all, it is well known that intelligence remains fixed for life from a young age."

"This approach towards intelligence and the way we fulfill our innate potential is superficial," Mario responded before continuing. "When we learn languages, arithmetic, music and sports, we train our brain. It's well known that the number of connections between the brain cells and their quality determines the complexity of the actions the brain is capable of performing. Training and stimulating the brain strengthens existing connections and even creates new ones. It is, therefore, possible to enhance one's abilities over time and improve the brain's performance. As we cope with more challenges, our brain develops. This is why here, on the west side of Mindset Land, many individuals handle a wide variety of interests at the same time and are not afraid to dare and leave their comfort zones."

"So, does that mean that everyone here believes they can succeed in whatever they choose if only they practice, work hard and apply themselves?" I asked.

"No, definitely not… We have a positive yet realistic idea of our abilities, and we're well aware of the fact that an individual neither can nor should expect to be equally good at all things. As far as we are concerned, success is our ability to act resolutely and invest our efforts in order to learn something new and develop. For this reason, failure is also a learning opportunity."

While listening to him, I wondered if he really meant what he said about failure. I have heard so many sentences such as "failure is an inseparable part of success" in my life. But, in fact, it is obvious to everyone that these sentences don't offer any comfort when you actually fail. However, Mario sounded very convinced to me...

"Excuse me for asking, Mario, but aren't you idealizing failure? According to you, it sounds like we should all aspire to fail – in order to learn and grow…"

"No, no one likes to fail," Mario answered, "But it seems to me that what you call failure, my friend, is not what I call failure. Your criterion for success or failure is the result, the bottom line. To us, the process is what counts, and 'failure' is to remain stagnant in one place – even if that place is a good and prestigious one. Failure is the unwillingness or inability to invest effort in order to realize your potential. Failure is stagnation and the lack of persistence when facing challenges.

"Therefore, even if you did accomplish some goals, we wouldn't consider it a success if you did it through a wrong or fixed-minded process that wasn't accompanied by any development, effort or learning on your behalf. To us, success is the ability to meet challenges in order to expand our horizons and grow."

"If you're telling me that, in your eyes, success is not measured by results, then there is definitely a gap between our cultures," I said.

"Probably," Mario replied. "I don't know the country you come from. But if it's similar to other developed countries, I guess it's a society that worships quick and superficial performance and doesn't endorse gradual and profound processes.

"I'm very proud of the place I grew up in and the values I

was raised on. From a young age, we were taught that through desire and effort, it is possible to nurture skills and personality, and to be more successful. We never received excessive praise for our personalities, since that kind of recognition produces dependency and adversely affects the willingness to strive and work hard for a goal or objective. What we did get as children, and passed on to ours, was the encouragement to work hard and make an effort. We believe that this is the key to a growth mindset and to realizing our potential."

"And how do you know when you've realized your full potential?"

"Maybe I will never know. But between you and me, what does it matter? It's obvious that it is impossible to predict where each of us will be years from now, and neither is it important, as long as will, persistence and determination exist. We try a wide variety of things and dare to take chances, and this promotes us. Both children and adults are filled with passion for learning, development and challenges. They overcome their disadvantages rather than hide them. To us, life is a journey – every day we evolve and become stronger, more talented and more competent."

"But don't you care if you are really talented in a particular area, an area on which you should totally focus?" I wondered, "After all, apart from your subjective experiences, there certainly is an objective reality. Or isn't there?"

"We can tell where we stand through our readiness to receive honest feedback from our environment. As we provide each other with constructive comments, we get to know our strengths and weaknesses. We are capable of evaluating our abilities, skills and performance. This knowledge serves us as a development tool. Of course, it also helps us to stay focused and realistic, and not to overestimate ourselves.

"I have an excellent example from the world of medicine. Dr. Groopman studied in depth the factors that lead doctors to make mistakes. In his book 'How Doctors Think'[11] he analyzes the thinking patterns of doctors that lead to mistakes. He firmly stresses the importance of feedback for success, stating that 'studies show that expertise is largely acquired not only by sustained practice but by receiving feedback that helps you understand your technical errors and misguided decisions'."

"So, if you believe that you can grow and develop, that errors are an inseparable part of your path, and that the way to realize your potential is a journey rather than a destination, you will find it easy to accept the information provided by others – teachers and coaches, managers and colleagues – regarding your abilities."

Mario's speech moved me and led me to contemplate the different ways in which we try to understand the source of our mistakes, the language we use to describe them and the conclusions we reach. Suddenly, I realized that this reflection process is very superficial and technical, and is not characterized by a valuable learning process. It brought to my mind the time I was insensitive to Tami, my team member, or the circumstances that led to my replacement in the project with the Germans. I also thought back on decisions I had made in the past and tried to remember what led me to reach them.

So many times in the past I had stuck to what I knew and was familiar with, and only agreed to lead projects in which I knew that I could exhibit my stronger sides. When was the last time I had made any real effort to learn something new, on my own will? When was the last time I had actually left my comfort zone and dared to study a new field, even if it meant dealing with my weaknesses or with sides that I hadn't developed as much? For a long time, I have felt that my work, and frankly my personal life as well, were a series of tests in which I had to prove myself.

I know that we, professional leaders, find it hard to deal with failures. Most of us don't talk about them at all or, even worse, try to hide them. It's as if someone etched an equation into our software, according to which we are only supposed to succeed and show the world how talented we are. When was the last time I asked for honest feedback about my work from someone who I thought highly of? There's a good chance that according to the standards of Mindset Land, I would probably be considered a failure.

"In this regard," Rona joined in. "I'd like to emphasize that one of the most important things to do in any organization is to strengthen the principle of 'teaching instead of blaming' – when something goes wrong, it should be viewed as an opportunity to get better. When a mistake occurs, it should be viewed as a teachable moment. Like in many other fields, it seems that accountants and advisors have the habit of finding who is to blame when a mistake takes place, rather than turning it into a learning process."

"Indeed," said Mario. "I definitely agree with that. I think more organizations should adopt this approach. Even more so – one of the capabilities that are characteristic of exceptional leaders is the process of giving feedback[12]. After setting clear expectations for their teams, these leaders give clear and decisive feedback in a way that is open, respectful and can be learned from. In addition, they offer themselves up for the criticism of their teams and express an openness to receive their feedback in return.

"Remember Michael," Mario added with a warm and confident smile, "In the new world that has evolved, the most important thing is to 'stay in the arena' – to live, to challenge yourself and to continue developing in the various fields that are important to your success. And even if you don't succeed in doing so at first, remember that at least you're there in the arena. Most of your friends aren't even there because, after all, it's much more convenient and safe not to be.

"There are five types of people who remain outside the arena. First, there's the blind type, those who don't even see that something has changed and try to convince everyone that what was true in the past will continue to be true in the future. Then there's the hesitant type, those who ask themselves 'to be or not to be' and fear to leave their comfort zone. And then, of course, there's the critical type, who will always tell you what you're doing wrong and what you could have done differently, and who will always explain why things don't apply to their world. Next, comes the cynical type, those who hate everyone and everything and wait for you to get struck by the first blow so they can tell you 'I told you to stay off the arena' with satisfaction. Finally, there's the perfectionist type, those who won't jump into the arena until they've read fifty studies and are certain that it's absolutely safe – and, obviously I'm not talking here about professional aspects that require extensive examination before adopting innovative processes[13].

"Let me end with a quote from Theodore Roosevelt:[14] *'It is not the critic who counts; not the man who points out how the strong man stumbles, or where the doer of deeds could have done them better. The credit belongs to the man who is actually in the arena, whose face is marred by dust and sweat and blood; who strives valiantly; who errs, who comes short again and again, because there is no effort without error and shortcoming; but who does actually strive to do the deeds; who knows great enthusiasms, the great devotions; who spends himself in a worthy cause; who at the best knows in the end the triumph of high achievement, and who at the worst, if he fails, at least fails while daring greatly, so that his place shall never be with those cold and timid souls who neither know victory nor defeat.'*

"And with this, Michael, it is time to continue," Rona interrupted. "We still have to make it to the other side of the city, the east side. And to get there, we'll have to cross the river by boat."

We said goodbye to Mario and proceeded to the pier on the riverbank.

***

As we reached the river, I was astounded by its flow and width, the floating plants along the bank and the old water mill. We saw ditches with ancient wooden bridges and were surrounded by merry fishermen and bathers of all ages. Everything seemed so full of life, and yet so calm.

We hired a small boat to take us to the opposite bank, and throughout the entire cruise I thought about Mario's words – the most important things are the investment of effort, learning and development. What does that mean to me?

About 10 minutes later we were standing on the opposite

river bank. The fishermen and bathers were here as well, but the atmosphere was less pleasant. We got off the boat and marched from the pier until we reached a main street paved with stone, with buildings that were surprisingly alike. We saw simple looking churches, entrances to subway stations and many industrial buildings. The streets were clean, but they lacked grace. The uniformity was also evident in the residential buildings and in the appearance of the people, who looked as if they were cast from a single mold. They all wore dark clothes and seemed troubled and self-centered. Their facial expressions were similar and monotonous. I looked at the billboards and saw posters advertising a single movie and a single show, a striking paucity compared to the richness and cultural diversity on the other bank.

I walked around, feeling that we had gone from a dynamic and vivid place to a stagnant place that got stuck in the past. I asked Rona if we were in the older part of the city.

Rona smiled, "Actually, this side is newer. Surprising, isn't it? We're on our way to meet a local guide to get some background on the culture and history of the locals. You can ask him anything."

After walking through drab streets, we reached a coffee shop where a tour guide who went by the name of Tom was waiting for us. The coffee shop belonged to a local chain, a kind of 'drink & go' which was very different from the intimate and pleasant coffee shops on the opposite bank. Rona, who sensed that I was uncomfortable, said, "Michael, you can ask Tom whatever crosses your mind about this place. This is why he's here."

Since Tom looked like a person who wasn't enthusiastic about his work and would gladly be doing something else, I politely asked him how many years he had been doing his job. He smiled at me and said, "Too many."

"Don't you enjoy your work?" I asked.

"Well, tour guiding was never my dream job," he answered.

"And what is your dream job, if I may ask?" I asked further.

"Since I was a child, my great passion was animals," Tom said, and by the look on his face, I felt that he appreciated the interest I was taking in his life. "I always dreamed of becoming a veterinarian. But, in order to be accepted to a veterinary school here, one has to pass difficult exams. I never applied because the odds were that I would never pass them."

I was surprised by the ease with which he gave up his dream. "Why weren't you more persistent?" I asked. "And, even if you had failed, couldn't you retake the tests?"

"It's interesting you should ask this," He answered, "because a friend of mine, who has similar skills to mine, applied once and failed. Then he studied for the tests for an entire year and passed them the second time. Today, he's indeed a successful veterinarian."

"So, why couldn't you do what he did? What's the difference between the two of you?"

"The difference between us is that when he was a child, my friend moved with his parents to the west side of Mindset Land." Tom smiled ironically and explained, "You see, geographically, there is just a river between the two parts of this land, but mentally, there is an ocean between us. The west side is a place where you can always get a second chance."

"Please explain this," I asked.

"Here, on the east side of Mindset Land, we believe that all people are born with a certain amount of intelligence and talent which remains constant throughout life. When they're in elementary school, young children receive an evaluation from their teachers regarding their abilities – their talent and professional orientation. These assessments rely mainly on ability tests according to which the children and their parents will make their decisions. My teachers thought that I wasn't born with the skills to be a veterinarian because I never excelled in life sciences."

"But what about effort and hard work?" Mario's speech came back to me. "Didn't your parents and teachers take these into account, as a means for success?"

"Here we believe that you either have it or you don't," Tom said with a bitter smile on his face. "If you don't, it's a lost cause. You won't be able to change the direction that your life is bound to take."

"This is the exact opposite of the concept of growth, in which they believe on the opposite side of the river," I noted.

"True, it is completely different. They also believe that innate talent is important, but it simply isn't the most important factor for success. They argue that each and every one of us has individual strengths and that one can develop and achieve almost anything with hard work, training and effort. The sky is the limit; that's their motto."

"So what is considered success around here?" I asked curiously.

"That's an interesting question, and the basis of everything. Here, success is measured by the result. If we demonstrate our abilities and talents in a noticeable and measurable way right from the beginning, we will be empowered by the environment."

"And do you have successful people who have made it, like on the other side?"

"We do, but very few of them. If you don't stand out with extraordinary talent, you won't even try, because it's obvious you can't be accomplished like those few stars. Those who do succeed are at the top of their category. When they are at the peak of their success, you can easily recognize them. Whether athletes, musicians or business people – when they're at the top, they're sure that they are the closest thing to God. In view of their success, they act arrogantly and disrespectfully toward others.

"But what's really sad is that their success doesn't last very long in many cases. Once reality changes and they have to do things differently or to invest effort in new directions, something happens to them. They give up and start to decline."

"How do you explain their inability to adjust to reality?" I asked.

At this point, Rona stepped into the conversation. "By the sound of it, they expect everything around them to change back so that they can recreate their success. But they don't take the time to look at themselves – at their own contribution to their decline and at what they should do to recreate their success. After all, being so talented, they can't possibly be the problem..."

Tom nodded in assent and said, "There's another factor keeping the most successful ones from investing effort to maintain their success. Here, we worship extraordinary talents and abilities. Effort is perceived as contrary to natural talent: talent is innate, and it is yours for good. That's why it's believed that if you are truly talented, you don't need to work hard and sweat.

"Failure takes those who have succeeded by surprise and exposes their weaknesses, which were mostly unknown until then, even to themselves. If you've been glorified by your environment throughout your entire life – a setback or temporary failure means that you are not so talented, after all. It means that you should make way for those who really are. From this point onward, two factors lead to a state of disability: fear of coping with another failure, and fear that people will see you're putting in effort and deduce that you're actually less talented than they thought.

"And this is the most difficult thing – to see all those fallen stars. It's one thing not to be successful from the start. But to turn into a star and then to have others figure out you aren't a prodigy becomes a terrible fall for the individual and his family, one that can be remembered for a long time. This is why most of those stars will do everything they can to prevent others from seeing that they sometimes slip up, experience difficulties or need to work hard. Here, on this side of Mindset Land, the fear of failure is much greater than the desire to succeed."

At this point, I couldn't restrain myself. I asked Tom how he explained the immense gap between the two parts of the land. "The conceptual difference between you and them is enormous and manifested in all areas of life – education, culture, construction, behavior and even external appearance. How is it possible? Where does it come from?"

Rona smiled and said, "To me, this is the key question. This is also the reason I chose to begin our journey here, in Mindset

Land. Tom, I would like to tell Michael the story because it inspires and moves me time and time again."

Smiling, Tom nodded, and Rona continued.

"You should understand it very well as it is very similar to the changes that your profession is going through. Many leaders who were the rising stars in the previous century, deep down, do understand that their profession has changed. They know that they need to leave their comfort zones and develop other types of skills and competencies. Yet, many of them prefer things to stay the way they are. As a result, they ignore or discount the traumatic changes on the horizon and stick to their comfort zones.

"Mindset Land initially began on the other side of the river, the west side, where our tour began. The way they lived, as well as their beliefs and values, were very much as they are here today. They sanctified talent, believing that the innate, intrinsic competencies are fixed at birth and cannot be changed, thus labeling children according to anticipated fields of profession and interest at a very young age.

"One day, a new teacher, Veronica, arrived at the leading school in town. They say that she came from another land. Veronica brought an innovative educational concept, which was contradictory to the common concept in Mindset Land. Veronica believed that valuing innate qualities alone and labeling the children according to them narrowed their ability to succeed in life. She also believed that every individual had a variety of different competences, which continuously grew and evolved throughout life.

"Where she came from, she had wonderful professors. One of them was Howard Gardner, who developed the theory of multiple intelligences and expanded the traditional concept of intelligence, arguing that each and every one of us has a unique composition of three forms of intelligence.[15] Another of her teachers, Robert Sternberg, talked about successful intelligence, a combination of several components of intelligence.[16] According to this theory, one needs to combine and use the aspects of all those components.

"With such notions in mind, she came to the fixed educational system in Mindset Land. She found that the students were taught to think, talk and act alike. All students were required to learn the same subjects, and all were measured by the same tools.

"Since they believed that their skills were innate and fixed, children who were not considered 'smart' by the system were thought of as having limited ability. They were not invested in, and no one expected much of them. Children whose parents and teachers didn't believe in their abilities also stopped believing in themselves. They didn't work hard since they thought they would never be able to change and become smarter. Veronica found it awful that the teachers and the parents didn't believe in their children's abilities. Their low grades were a ticket to a slow path of life.

"The high grades of the 'smart' students got them on the fast track to success. Ironically, they also felt that they didn't need to work hard – because they were talented, no matter what. And so, at a certain point, they stopped making progress.

"Veronica honestly believed that individuals could develop their skills through effort and hard work. In fact, she started the revolution on her own: she decided to change this situation, contacted her former professors and constructed a unique curriculum with them.

"She instilled in her students the awareness that intelligence appeared in a variety of forms and expressions, and that talent alone wasn't enough to succeed. Constant work and practice were necessary. She showed them that some children were better in sports, others were talented musicians, and still others were better in logic, language, spatial orientation or social skills. She taught them that each and every one of them had different abilities that could be developed.

"Above all, she argued that your real challenge was to find your own talents, work hard and not give up, even when you encounter an obstacle. In her pleasant way, Veronica convinced the children that it was possible to view obstacles as gifts that assist us to develop and improve, and that these hardships and challenges teach us much more than constant success. You can imagine the reaction of the parents of those children as they understood the content that was being taught at school."

"I bet they were pleased. The rationale seems so correct," I said.

"A small group of parents did understand the rare opportunity these children were given and supported the new spirit that Veronica introduced into the school. But there was also strong opposition to her method from a larger group of parents. Veronica's name became prominent, and she was the hot topic in people's conversations for a long time, a subject of admiration or objection – depending on who you asked."

"I can't understand the objections of these parents. After

all, as she promoted their children, they must have seen the results."

"True," said Tom, who rejoined the conversation. "The students benefited from her, big time; and surprisingly, not just the 'weaker' children, but also the 'smarter' ones. Although they were getting high grades, many of them were actually afraid and even anxious due to the high expectations from them.

"Despite the criticism, Veronica wouldn't give up. For instance, during the first few months, she refused to submit the children to the school's Growth and Effectiveness Measures so that they wouldn't be prematurely labeled. She also believed in opening diverse learning channels and occupied the children with physical activity, singing and group dynamics.

"Many parents considered this a waste of precious time. There was a serious debate among the parents, and the argument heated up. Those who opposed her demanded to go back to the methods used thus far. They argued that Veronica's activity would impair the children's achievements and cause the school's level to drop. Those who supported her felt persecuted. However, since the school principal was supportive of her, a large group left angrily and started a settlement on the east side of the river. Since then, the people have been divided into two distinct groups, with an almost complete separation between the two sides."

I thought of Veronica, a single teacher with a mission, who was able to inspire so many individuals and change their reality. It reminded me of Jane, my eighth-grade teacher, who actually changed my life. She was the first one to believe in me, to look at me and see something beyond what everybody else saw. She became my homeroom teacher two years after I immigrated to Israel from Argentina with my family. By that time, I already had a reputation at school of a silent and introverted boy. At that point, the teachers had given up and didn't try to call on me, after two years of unsuccessful attempts to make me participate in class. I had no problem understanding them, but I was afraid the children would make fun of my accent. Besides, I was secretly hoping that if my parents saw that I wasn't adjusting, they would do an about-face. I wished we would all return to Argentina and I would be reunited with the friends I left behind.

Jane identified my abilities and made me feel that she believed in me. She taught me to have faith in myself, to progress and to grow. But now, in retrospect, despite all the progress I made, I think that my success was only measured with grades. I never realized that just as investing efforts improves success in school, it might also bring about the same consequences in other areas of life such as relationships, business abilities, or coping with changes. In these areas, I had always thought exactly like the fixed-minded individuals here – you either have it, or you don't. Actually, come to think of it, I believe that most of us in my department think like that regarding subjects not related to our professional work. I recalled many conversations with John in which all his attempts to show me that, with effort, it was possible to develop interpersonal skills and adaptability, had gone by me unnoticed.

***

"How about we go back to the west side of the city where we started our visit? We'll stroll around the piazzas. There are some more people I would like to tell you about. Some of them you might not recognize, but you will recognize some others as famous and successful."

I was thrilled at the invitation to leave the gloomy atmosphere behind and go back to the nicer and more interesting side of the city. We thanked Tom and sailed back to the other bank. Rona showed me an old picture of a child and asked, "Do you recognize this tall boy holding a basketball?"

"Not really..."

"His name is Michael Jordan. Does that ring a bell?"

"Sure, I know him as an adult player, but I didn't recognize him as a child."

"What do you think of him?"

"I think he's the best basketball player of all time. He has an innate phenomenal talent, and you won't find another player to match his abilities today."

"I agree with the second part of your observation; there's no player today who can match him. However, I disagree about the role of his phenomenal talent in his success. Clearly, he was born with great talent, but this isn't the entire story. I want to share some facts about him that might be new to you. Did you know that he was practically cut from the basketball team as a high school sophomore[17] when he was 15? His coach argued that he wasn't fit to be a team player and assigned him to the junior varsity team."

"That's hard to believe," I was surprised.

"Also, he didn't make the cut the first time he tried to join the basketball team at the University of North Carolina. As a result, he didn't meet the professional standard required by scholarship applicants. And, believe it or not, before he became a superstar, he didn't make the cut on two NBA teams."

"Are you sure?"

"I'm certain. And do you know what his mother said to him when the coach cut him off the team? She said he wasn't disciplined enough and didn't practice sufficiently. She said that if he took himself seriously and practiced he would improve and become a master. So he took her advice seriously and started practicing with determination – getting up at five o'clock every morning and practicing as hard as he could. In fact, in all the years he played basketball he never stopped practicing. He became the most devoted NBA player, who practiced even after games, whether his team won or lost. The assistant coach of the Chicago Bulls once said that he is a genius constantly perfecting his genius quality. When asked how he does it, Michael Jordan simply answered, 'I just keep throwing the ball.'"

"And he who throws more, scores more. This is obvious," I said.

"Are you familiar with the 10,000 hours rule?"

"No..."

"This is a rule formulated by the Canadian writer Malcolm Gladwell in his book *Outliers*.[18] The rule states that in order to achieve mastery in a field, one must practice for about 10,000 hours – which may take 5 to 10 years. When we see an extraordinary athlete, a Nobel Prize laureate or a fabulous musician, we do not see what happens backstage. We don't see the many hours of effort they put in, the sweat and the disappointments they experienced in order to reach their greatest achievements. We think that such people are simply geniuses or lucky. But it is obvious that high-level personal ability and even genius quality are not a guarantee for success. They are most certainly a good thing to start with, but it's impossible to reach extraordinary achievements without hard work and without risking failure. As Michael Jordan said when asked what the secret of his success was – 'I failed over and over in my life and that is why I succeed.'"

"I have another example of the importance of hard work on the road to success," Rona said. "At the music academy in Berlin, teachers were asked to divide their violin students into three groups. The first was the group of elite performers, students who had a high potential of becoming world-renowned musicians. The second group included those who were considered 'good' or professional. In the third group were the less able performers that were actually designated to become music teachers. All the students were asked an identical question: 'How much time did you practice throughout your career since you first held a violin?'"

"It turned out that during the initial stages of their studies, when they were about five years old and started to play, they all practiced for about the same number of hours. But as the years went by, substantial gaps were formed. And so, by the time they were 20 years old, the 'stars' had accumulated about ten thousand hours of practice, while the 'good' violinists about eight thousand. The future music teachers had only four thousand hours of practice.

"A book called 'Grit'[19] that reinforces this concept has recently been published and quickly became a world bestseller. It was written by Dr. Angela Duckworth from the University of Pennsylvania. When Dr. Duckworth began her career, she was a consultant in one of the world's leading strategic firms. At some point, she decided to leave consulting and engage in what she thought of as one of the most important professions in the world – the teaching profession. From there, she continued her studies and did a Ph.D. in psychology. One question interested her very much – what leads people to succeed in life? Dr. Duckworth found that the answer can be found by studying grit and self-control, two attributes that are distinct from IQ and yet powerfully predict success and well-being.

"Her research clearly indicates that what brings people to succeed in life is not necessarily a high IQ or an extraordinary talent. Among the most important capabilities for success are a unique combination of passion and long-term perseverance. Those who possess it are able to self-regulate and postpone their need for positive reinforcement while working diligently on a task.

"You see, it doesn't matter what the occupation in question is – sports, chess, ice skating, science or teaching – those who reached the top are those who have invested many hours and worked much harder than anyone else."

"If the crucial role of investment and determination is so well known, how come the inhabitants of the gloomy, eastern side of this land don't adopt this attitude?" I asked.

"As the years go by, there is a slow immigration of people to the western side. But many still stay on the fixed-minded eastern side and are either not interested or incapable of opening up to new perceptions. It's possible that they are afraid to make the effort and leave their comfort zone. These people are deeply set in their fixation, but you and I can still make a choice.

"You have a choice, Michael. You can choose which bank of

the river you want to live in: whether to stay fixated in your abilities and skills or to adopt a growth mindset. By choosing a growth mindset you choose a path by which hard work and effort will bring about achievements in all areas, even those in which you are currently less capable."

She is right, I thought to myself. It was up to me – I had to choose whether to keep dragging around in my comfort zone, retaining what I have without taking any risks, or to open up to challenges and risks as opportunities to progress and grow. I recalled my accounting studies and felt frustrated. Most of the classes focused on the technical aspects of the profession, and didn't even touch on the all-important issue of our mindset.

I suddenly remembered a conversation I had with John several months ago, after he had taken part in a partners' meeting. He told me that many of the partners he encountered wanted to prove, to others and to themselves, that they knew all the answers. He claimed that they were managed by quite a bit of ego and an enormous fear of failure and making mistakes, and no less important – a fear of being perceived as incompetent. This may be an exaggeration, but now it made a little more sense to me…

"Tell me, Rona, how is it that so many leaders aren't really familiar with these concepts? And why isn't anyone addressing such an important and dominant issue?"

"Some people deal with mindsets, the most prominent of which is a highly distinguished professor from Stanford University, Carol Dweck. I told you about her just before we boarded the plane. She's been dealing with this issue for more than 20 years."

"Why haven't I heard of her?"

"Her work is gradually becoming more widely recognized. Her groundbreaking book on Mindset[20] generated considerable interest from readers, and is highly important to me. In this book, you can learn a lot about mindsets and their influence on a variety of aspects of our lives. This book will undoubtedly convince you that our mindset deeply influences our professional and personal achievements, differentiating those who achieve their goals from those who don't."

"I'll add it to my reading list," I said with a smile.

"Michael, do you know why the mindset is so critical, especially in the 21st century? It's because, as I told you, reality is constantly changing. For this reason, the existing repertoire that led us to success at a certain stage is insufficient in the next phase. As a result of this changing reality, the concept of leadership is also undergoing significant change. We will see more and more leaders who develop their skills through learning, throughout life, because this pattern of growth will lead to progress and success. Or, as John Kotter from Harvard argued in his book *Leading Change*[21] – changing the behavior of individuals is the most important challenge for organizations attempting to compete in a world dominated by changes and crises."

"When speaking of a growth mindset, and looking at a wide variety of materials dealing with the challenges facing the accounting and advisory world in the 21st century, it seems to me that the successful advisors of the 21st century will have to adopt this kind of attitude regarding five different fields that are significant to their work. I call this model the 'Whole Advisor' model. Only leaders who hold a growth mindset attitude in these five fields will be able to create a reality in which our people will be extraordinary, our clients will always see a difference in us, and the public will trust us since we are valued by investors and respected in our profession."

"Why didn't you call it the 'Whole Accountant' model?" I asked. "After all, many of us still provide traditional accounting and audit work."

"As I see it, Michael, every accountant who works with clients in the 21st century must embrace the attitude and the skills of an advisor in order to provide his clients with any sort of value. But on the other hand, as an auditor, you must keep your independence of mind and appearance all the time. You must not compromise your professional judgment; always act with integrity and exercise objectivity and professional skepticism. This is the reason why your firm chose 'act with integrity' as one of its core values.

"Now, the first field, as you can see on the tablet I gave you, is the professional field. I am sure most advisors will agree that any advisor must have a growth mindset, professionally speaking, though not all of them do.

"The second field is Technology and Innovation. Advisors of the 21st century will need to be smart users of new technologies that enter the world of professional service firms from fields like communications, automation, and artificial intelligence. From my experience, a significant portion of accountants and advisors fear the use of such new technologies and are not prepared for them. But they must understand that they have no choice, as this is the direction in which the accounting and advisory world is headed.

"The third field is Leadership. The accounting profession is one that affords partners and directors a lot of autonomy. But to become the clear choice of their strategic clients and most talented employees, they will have to exhibit leadership and management skills. First of all, they need to think of themselves as inspirational leaders. And it starts on the inside. Leaders need to find, deep within themselves, their own personal vision and their own sense of true purpose in the profession. Vision and a sense of purpose are critical factors in creating endless passion and preventing burnout. In addition, like in the past, they also need to have managerial capabilities, since they have to manage their teams, their clients, their time and of course their career.

"The fourth field is Emotional Intelligence. Nowadays, whether employees or leaders, accountants must believe that they can develop their own soft skills, which are so very critical to their personal success. This is especially crucial when it comes to employees' engagement, passion and grit, as well as leading change, building relationships with clients and becoming a trusted advisor.

"And last but not least, comes the field of Business Value Proposition. I know that many accountants and even some advisors don't feel that business is a natural part of their profession. When I talk about mindset in this context, I mean that they need to develop a winning personal value proposition in the market and to be experts in the industries that they operate in. They need to know how local and global trends may affect their client's success in the coming years, to hold a global mindset and to bring solutions from the global firm. Of course, they should also know what are the most important issues on the c-suite table, which keep them up at night. Whenever possible, they should bring them valuable and creative solutions to these issues. They don't have to stay at the office all day long. Rather, they should invest the time and effort in order to build a meaningful network and to be the trusted advisors of the CEOs and owners of companies in their industry. In addition, to be considered 'top advisors' they should be game changers and thought leaders.

"The accountants and advisors who can do all these will

obviously be those who are not afraid of mistakes and temporary failure and, therefore, are guided by a growth mindset. They will become lifelong learners – professionals who learn throughout their entire life. Better yet, they will be the ones to promote the constant improvement of all the products and services offered by their firm.

"Our conversation reminds me of a lecture which was given by professor Laura Empson from London's Cass Business School. She wrote a very important book about leadership in professional firms by the name of *'Leading Professionals: Power, Politics, and Prima Donnas.'* She also has a very interesting talk on YouTube by that name, in which she talks about the fact that true power in professional firms belongs to people who control access to keys resources. In our case, we are talking about valuable clients' relationships, specialist technical expertise and strong reputation in the marketplace. You can understand by now that no one can create this type of power without the main skills and competencies of the Whole Advisor.

"Michael, it's important for me to emphasize that when leaders learn about growth mindset and fixed mindset, they become more aware of opportunities for self-development. They also become more open to challenges in the five fields of the 'Whole Advisor' model and more resilient when facing obstacles on the way. It is extremely important that leaders should tell their team members that they believe in them and in their ability to expand their talent, if they would put in the time and energy.[22] This should be done while sharing with the team the research on growth mindset and the plasticity of the brain. And I especially recommend the works of Professor Dweck and Dr. Michael Merzenich. You can watch Dr. Merzenich online. Try to find his excellent TED talk titled *'Growing evidence of brain plasticity'*, for example. Leaders also need to share with their team members some of their personal stories about high performing professionals who were dedicated to their jobs and developed skills and competencies over time."

Thinking once again of my conversation with John, I suddenly remembered that he had also said that accounting schools should change their goals and their teaching and evaluation methods in order to create accountants who are lifelong learners. He said that the next generation of accountants needed training that would lead them to be more creative and innovative, in order to better understand the needs of their clients and find new solutions for them. He also claimed that the education of young accountants had to inspire them to be curious professionals, in addition to them being knowledgeable and effective professionals. He went on to say that when we are committed to a growth mindset and to innovation and when we are willing to approach the accounting education with an open mind and fresh eyes, the only limit is our own imagination. I suddenly realized that he actually spoke about the 'Whole Advisor' model, even though he didn't call it by that name.

"It seems really challenging," I said. "I have to admit, I don't think there are many accountants like the 'Whole Advisor' in my immediate surroundings."

"Michael, the idea isn't that every accountant will be required to demonstrate level 10 capabilities in every field that makes up the 'Whole Advisor' model. But both of us can agree that we don't want to see directors or partners whose level of performance is a 5 or 6, out of 10, in two or three of the fields."

"I understand," I replied. "But Rona, what will they actually do? How will they develop?"

"Well, I agree that it's a challenging process that requires quite a bit of effort," Rona answered. "The first thing they will need to do is identify their strengths and weaknesses in these five fields – professionalism, technology and innovation, leadership, emotional intelligence, and business value proposition. Then, they have to set challenging goals for themselves in order to improve and develop their weaknesses, formulate plans for meeting these goals and take part in different programs that develop their capabilities, both within the firm and outside of it.

"They will need to proactively seek feedback from their managers, colleagues, employees, consultants and clients. Throughout the way, they will need to conduct processes of reflection and mirroring in order to examine their progress in each field. And if necessary, they will have to set further goals for themselves. An important point to note is that every advisor can perform such a process on his or her own, but if the head of the department or any other partner leads such a process, the chances of it succeeding substantially increase."

"Sounds like an excellent plan," I smiled at Rona.

"Before we move on," Rona smiled back, "I would like you to look at your tablet and see the summary I sent you."

We continued touring the lively streets, and in my head, I heard myself repeating the mantra "people do not change" in various conversations with John and Martha. I felt a wave

In the changing world of today, the successful managers will be the ones who...

- Understand that as leaders, they have to change.
- Adopt a growth mindset attitude.
- Understand that practice, learning and development are a part of their work.
- Evaluate their performance and skills effectively and work hard in order to develop.
- Internalize that change entails a certain amount of risk, but that risk management is anyway part of their job as leaders.
- Realize that change includes learning: if you do not learn, you will become irrelevant.
- Remember that change must come with effort: if you do not put in sufficient effort, you won't be a part of the game.

of embarrassment and shame. I understood why Rona said that our first destination was of crucial importance in our journey and that no significant process could take place without it. I consciously decided to try to adopt the attitude I saw on the river bank at which I first arrived, and to remind myself that inquisitiveness, determination, hard work, experimentation and practice were valuable skills for success.

As if reading my mind, Rona said, "Michael, I think that any firm that wants to continue to succeed in the 21ˢᵗ century has to understand that leaders need to support intellectual curiosity, risk taking, and creativity – the characteristics of accountants with a growth mindset. Like other hotbeds of innovation, firms must have a high tolerance for 'renegades' – the kind of people who are dissatisfied with the status quo and are always looking for better ways of doing things. No firm can be successful unless its people are free to learn from their mistakes. This doesn't mean that such advisors are indifferent to clients, but rather the opposite – clients are very important to them, and they are highly motivated to provide them with the best value proposition as possible."

I thought of the famous Churchill quote my great-uncle Jacob used to say all the time – "*Success consists of going from failure to failure without loss of enthusiasm*" – and I could already feel my own excitement building in expectation of our next destination.

Suddenly, I heard Rona saying, "Michael, we must go to the airport now. Our flight leaves in two hours." At the airport gate, Rona told me that our next destination was a fascinating land, a kingdom led by *King M the Fourth*.

Needless to say, his name sounded quite peculiar to me…

3
Artgineer Land

The landing was smooth. The plane touched down, and I didn't even feel the queasiness that I often experience during landings.

As we left the airport, I saw the strangest and most surreal sight I have ever seen. All the people on the street had their heads tilted! They were walking, talking, drinking coffee and reading the newspaper with their heads tilted at quite a sharp angle. This fascinating and bizarre sight is hard to describe – you just have to see it to believe it! The only normal-looking ones were the children, who had only a slight tilt of the head or none at all.

"What's going on here?" I asked Rona, "An entire land of people with tilted heads? Is it a genetic neck problem affecting an entire population?"

"Not at all, Michael, this is not a genetic flaw, but a physical expression of a brain preference. Now, take a good look at the people to see the nuances. Notice that some of the heads are tilted to the right while others to the left. Some are tilted by only a slight angle while others by a sharper one."

Truth be told, I had noticed these differences, but I didn't give it much thought. So, what was this brain preference that Rona spoke about? And why was it so noticeably expressed in the physical stature of these people? How come a slight tilt in childhood became sharper as they grew up? And finally, why were some of the heads tilted at a sharper angle than others?

All of these questions preoccupied me. "Do you think we appear strange to the locals, just as they appear strange to us?" I asked. Rona smiled and nodded.

"So, what's the difference between people with a tilt to the right and those with a tilt the left?" I yelled in order to make myself heard over the noisy crowd that surrounded us.

Rona gestured that she couldn't hear me because of the tumult in the streets. Children and adults were walking in the streets and the atmosphere seemed festive. The coffee shops and restaurants were flooded with diners. It looked as if everyone was having a good time and I wondered if they were celebrating a local tradition.

But I also sensed that it wasn't just the noise that kept Rona from answering me. She must have wanted me to take in the situation on my own. I continued looking at the passersby, trying to figure out what was really happening in this strange land.

As we were walking in the street, carried away by the masses, we heard there would be a ceremony in 15 minutes in the town square, by the king's palace. The very existence of a monarchy in a place that has such a modern appearance surprised me, but I gave up the attempt to figure it out. Instead, I tried to focus and find a way through the masses hurrying toward the town square.

A great crowd was gathered in front of the palace, and giant plasma screens in the adjacent streets enabled the masses to see what was going on. Loud applause rang out everywhere as the announcer invited *King M the Fourth* to take the stage. The king, who looked as if he came out of an old fairytale book, opened the ceremony with a warm voice, filled with enthusiasm:

My beloved people! As you all know, our kingdom, which was once prosperous and successful, is currently in distress. We have tried our best to overcome the difficulties, but our attempts have failed in view of the frequent global crises and rising unemployment. At this point in time, it appears that the survival of our current practices and traditions does not stand much of a chance. Therefore, after days and nights of consulting with our best experts, I can do nothing but be as responsible as I can, and turn the kingdom over to new hands.

I can imagine your feelings upon hearing this news, and I admit that, personally, I too am filled with a fear of walking toward the unknown. But at such moments, it is important to remember that we are not the first to deal with this kind of situation and probably other lands will follow. My advisors have searched the books and found out that such dramatic events occur about once in two hundred years, and it is happening now. I call upon all of you to be united, to accept the difficulty as a challenge and to hope that the change will be for the best. We have reached the stage in which we must try to remember how to use the additional parts of the brain, the ones that each of us has neglected over the years. Therefore, I am turning the kingdom over to the Artgineers.

"He means those who make use of all four parts of the brain!" Rona yelled towards me. I never really took the issue of Right Brain and Left Brain too seriously and often treated it as nonsense. But now I wondered how the brain had suddenly attained two additional parts... What was going on here and what is an Artgineer?

The crowd in the streets was excited, and shouts of "Long live the King!" sounded everywhere.

"Let's go to the nearby university, we can talk there," Rona proposed.

We made our way through the crowd and reached the campus, where we sat at a coffee shop, enjoying relative peace and quiet. I sat back in my chair, took a sip of coffee and asked Rona, "What did the king mean when he said that certain parts of the brain were neglected? And what does all of this have to do with their success?"

Rona took her time before answering me. "Do you remember the lessons from the journey to Mindset Land?"

I nodded.

"What is the most significant insight that you have from there?"

"I understand now that the people who will succeed in the 21st century will have a growth mindset which will enable them to adapt to the changing reality."

"True. This is indeed a necessary condition for success in the 21st century, but it's not a sufficient one. Because even those who do have a growth mindset still have to use all four parts of the brain in a harmonious manner, in order to succeed."

"And what are the four parts of the brain?" I asked.

"Soon, we'll hear a detailed explanation from a team of

leading brain researchers here at the university. But before meeting them, let's start from the basic model dividing the brain into two primary parts – left and right. According to this model, the left side of the brain is mostly responsible for precise activities such as logical thinking, language skills and identification of information. The right side of the brain, on the other hand, is mostly used for abstractions, identifying nuances and fitting information into bigger schemes. Therefore, individuals with a so-called left-brain tendency are rational and analytic: they rely on facts, numbers and details, people who check the applied aspect of things – the engineer type. Those with a right-brain tendency are driven by a vision. They are intuitive, inspirational, creative and verbal characters who look at the bigger picture – the artistic type."

"Is this division scientifically valid?" I wondered.

"Good question, and one that definitely reflects your brain tendency," Rona answered in an amused tone. "As you very well know, there is still much that we do not know about the brain. I have no doubt that if you ask neurobiologists, they'll have their reservations about the simplistic division of right-brain and left-brain. They will probably say that any complex cognitive behavior obliges us to use both parts of the brain. It is obvious that proper functioning is possible only when both parts of the brain act in cooperation.

"So, it appears to me that we should treat this division as if it were a metaphor for two types of thinking: the logical-linear way and the creative-intuitive way. Mostly, it is the way we prefer and nurture a particular kind of thinking that makes the difference. In this land, we can clearly see the bizarre physical expression of this division. If you look around, you will also see that individuals with a certain brain tendency prefer the company of those who are like them. They sit at the same places, share interests, tend to choose related occupations and, in most cases, they also choose partners with the same brain tendency."

"At the tennis club where I play on Fridays there is a group of accountants from another Big4 firm who only play amongst themselves," I remembered with amusement. "It always seemed ridiculous to me."

"Well, in fact, marriage between individuals with opposite brain tendencies is rare here in Artgineer Land. It is actually considered a form of mixed marriage. Even though children of such parents are known to be multi-disciplinary and extremely talented, they find it difficult to adapt socially, and this is the reason such cases occur only rarely. It appears that everyone wants to retain the familiar. They eventually educate their children according to the priorities and values that derive from their own brain tendency. Consequently, they search for a similar spouse. Parental investment in acquiring life skills characterized by one's own brain tendency is dominant, and thus, gradually, children resemble their parents."

"Fine," I said, "this explains why the head tilt of children is smaller and increases with age. But how do these two very different camps get along here, when the division is so distinct?"

"As you have heard from the king, his kingdom knew many years of prosperity. But who do you think were the people who held the leading and senior positions? And who do you think are those who enjoyed the highest incomes?"

"If this is anything like our world, those people are probably the ones who developed the left part of their brain."

"True. Throughout the past hundred years, there was a clear hierarchic structure. The ones at the top of the pyramid were those who were inclined to use the left part of their brain. Engineers, accountants, economists, lawyers and bankers held pure knowledge in their hands. They had an advantage where rational thinking was concerned. They were successful, and were placed at the head of the organizational ladder: they had high salaries, excellent working conditions, respect and prestige. Individuals with right-brain dominance went into professions such as teaching, counseling, social work and art. Some of them were able to get promoted, but the senior positions were never open to them, and the hegemony of those with a left-brain tendency was retained over the years."

"And then, what changed?"

"The change is related to the global process I mentioned – the shift from the knowledge era to the conceptual era and the creative era. In Artgineer Land, the signs of change appeared earlier than in the rest of the world as a result of the sharp divide that exists here between right-brain and left-brain people. There are almost no in-betweens. So, eventually, the management methods didn't endorse cooperation and collaboration. The work environment became less supportive and less inclusive. There was no creative development due to the emphasis on functionality. People became frustrated and felt unappreciated, which resulted in a gradual productivity decline. This crisis was topped with the relocation of some of the land's factories to countries where production is cheaper. Add to this the global economic instability, and there you have it: a kingdom in crisis."

"And what did the people do to emerge from the crisis?" I asked.

"There were attempts to heal the economy through local resources. But these attempts failed and the king decided to seek external help. He sent his advisors to review the literature, and they found a theory by an American researcher, Ned Herrmann, the Whole Brain Model,[23] which seemed to have been developed specially for them. Ned Herrmann was a physicist and musician who worked as a department head at General Electric. He coped with issues that affect this kingdom and, by the way, are a source of concern for executives everywhere: how to increase the productivity, motivation and creativity of their employees.

"The king's advisors wrote Herrmann a letter describing their crisis. The letter touched Herrmann and he sent a student of his, Peter, to try to help them find their way out of the crisis. Peter brought a vast amount of knowledge, which he had received from his teacher, and presented it to the experts from the Faculty of Brain Sciences.

"First, Herrmann relied on thorough studies about the lateralization of brain functions: the different specializations related to the left and right hemispheres of the brain. Notice that just as most of us have a dominant hand, foot or eye, we also have a dominant brain hemisphere. Naturally, in a pair of organs, the preference of one organ over the other also means more frequent use of it, increasing its performance in expert tasks. Similarly, the brain hemisphere which is more frequently used from a young age becomes dominant and strengthens throughout life."

"Fine," I interrupted, "I understand that according to his model it is possible to develop skills for all parts of the brain through practice, just like you develop your muscles.

But you haven't told me **what** the four parts of the brain actually are."

"That's because I wanted you to hear about them from Peter himself. I will only say that, based on his studies, Herrmann has added one more dimension to the lateral model of the right-brain and left-brain. The additional division results from the different specializations of the cerebral cortex and the limbic system. In general, the cerebral cortex plays a key role in cognitive functions, while the limbic system supports functions such as emotions, behavior and long-term memory. Thus, Herrmann outlines a four-quadrant model of the brain, with each quadrant resulting in a different thinking style and, accordingly, different reasoning skills and different styles of interaction with others. Additionally, our use of these four thinking styles shapes our mindset and our approach to solving diverse problems.

"Peter is nearby, in the Faculty of Brain Sciences. For years, he has been studying and teaching and is considered a senior lecturer. Let's go meet him and hear a more detailed explanation about the Whole Brain Model."

On our way to the faculty, as we passed through several areas in the university, it was apparent that most people here had their heads tilted to the left. I asked Rona if this attribute had become a screening tool for certain faculties, much like the SAT. Rona answered that this wasn't the case. "However, people did choose to apply to programs according to their brain tendency because they would rather study something that suits them, a profession that they will be good at."

Rona led me towards the Accounting Faculty. She wanted

to demonstrate how most of the students in my field had left-brain tendencies.

"You know, Rona," I said, "I must admit that I am overcome with a feeling of confusion and even a little sadness after learning about this model and discovering that most accounting students have such a one-sided predisposition. I feel it especially now that I understand the importance of having a vision, empathy and good interpersonal relationships in order to succeed as a leader in our profession. Most of all, I feel confused because this one-sided tendency most probably characterizes most partners and directors in our firm, including myself."

"I definitely get what you're saying," Rona replied, "and I have to admit that I often feel like you, especially because I care so much about your firm and the people who work there."

"I also notice that

We went up to the top floor of the building and met a large and heterogeneous crowd of students, attesting to the fact that the issue of brain preference occupied both camps. We knocked on the door and entered Peter's office. Peter was a large man in his fifties with long black hair. He gazed at me for a long time, smiling. "I look at you and remember the first time I came here. I assume this is the first time you've met individuals with tilted heads."

"Yes, the sight is both bizarre and fascinating," I answered.

"And the underlying brain mechanism is even more fascinating," Peter said. "I understand that your interest in the model of the four brain parts developed by my teacher brings you here, so come, let's have a seat."

After we sat down, I asked Peter whether he believed that

brain preference, thinking style, and their bizarre physical expression in the form of a tilted head were genetic or nurtured.

"I'll try to simplify it," Peter answered. "The brain tendency is a product of both nature and nurture. For years now, we have no longer been concerned with the quantification of the influences of heredity versus environment. Today, we focus on the practical aspect, on the influence of the environment. Children are born with a unique set of qualities and personality traits. Then, they are exposed to a certain reality through their parents, their teachers and their surroundings. As for the head tilt we observe in Artgineer Land, it seems to appear around the age of three or four, when the brain tendency is formed. No doubt, both you and I lean towards a certain brain tendency, which influences our abilities, our choices, our decision-making process, and our relationships with ourselves and our surroundings. Yet, it has never resulted in the physical expression that is so typical and evident in this land.

"Now, let's take a better look at the details of the Whole Brain Model," Peter said. He dimmed the lights, and on the screen appeared a table entitled "Ned Herrmann's Four Brain Styles".[24]

"I will spare you the theoretical background of the model. From my years of experience, I know that people get lost when faced with physiological explanations, which take us away from the point. The point is outlined in this table, or model map, which presents four thinking types and represents four different characters.

"Now, let's see how each of these four different characters

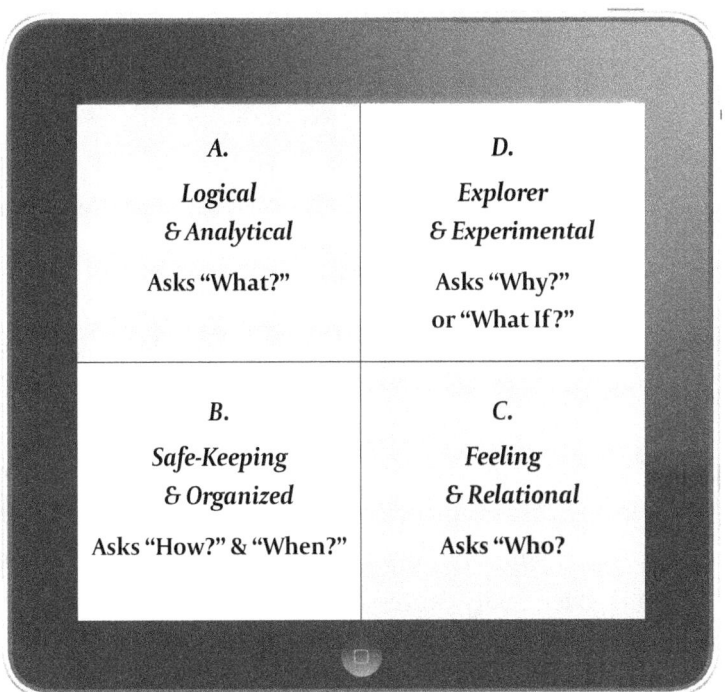

A.	D.
Logical *& Analytical*	*Explorer* *& Experimental*
Asks "What?"	Asks "Why?" or "What If?"
B.	C.
Safe-Keeping *& Organized*	*Feeling* *& Relational*
Asks "How?" & "When?"	Asks "Who?

would face a change, as directors or partners – what would their approach be and what questions would they ask?

"Clearly, Partner A is more logical and analytical. Focusing on facts and the bottom-line, he prefers numbers and charts. Seeking a realistic and clear vision of the process, he is critical and methodological. He enjoys problem-solving, debating and making things work. Finally, he controls processes by measuring performance and achievements.

"Partner B seeks order and sequential procedures. His approach to change processes is to organize them in terms of how and when. He focuses on getting the tasks done by carefully planning in advance. He might feel somewhat insecure during times of change since he prefers predictable circumstances in which he can rely on past experience and confirmed methods."

"Those are certainly the left-brain people, like many partners in the DPP, for example," I said.

"Exactly," Peter replied. "Now let's find out what characterizes right-brain partners."

"Well, as Rona told me earlier, I guess they are more emotional and sensitive, intuitive and creative."

"Indeed," Peter continued, "Partner C prefers to engage in dialogue about the change. He will focus on the team members and their roles, their feelings and relationships. Since he loves to help and mentor others, he will communicate the change and provide support. Throughout the process, he will act as a team player, easily expressing his feelings and encouraging others to do so. When facing problems, he will follow his instincts and view challenges as growth opportunities.

"Finally, rather than tightly controlling and planning the process in advance, Partner D prefers having multiple options, leaving room for intuition and improvisation. He prefers to focus on 'the big picture' and the vision of how things will eventually be. Being an explorer, he will ask questions such as 'why' and 'what if' and may easily break the rules and take risks.

"Now, try to think which character is dominant in you, Michael, or maybe it's a combination of two characters," Peter told me.

I thought about it for a minute. "I guess I am a type A... or maybe an AB," I said, "but I'm not sure, there are moments when I feel like a D..."

"That's very logical. Each of us has one or two dominant types. However, for most of us, the preferences aren't too rigid. Under certain circumstances, it is possible to expand them. This is the issue at hand – how to expand our skills and diversify our courses of action. Our research teams work day and night in order to build tools that enable individuals to develop all four parts of the brain."

"To what end? To improve the employees' productivity?" I asked.

"That's just a side benefit. Please note that knowing where we are located on the model map is a real asset on the personal level. It gives us an awareness of our strengths and weaknesses. It enables us to emphasize the development of dormant skills so that we'll be able to apply them when the time comes. Awareness of our mindsets allows us to maximize our personal skills through better communication with our surroundings and to obtain new problem-solving tools and effective learning methods."

"But why emphasize our weaknesses? Shouldn't we do the opposite?" I asked. "Isn't it better to focus on further developing our strengths for better performance?"

"If we focus on our strengths, our weaknesses will never improve," Peter replied. "Let me better answer your question with an example. Let's say that you're a manager with a left brain preference, as you suggested, a type A or B, or a combination of both. Say you have a group of 10 employees you have to lead through a complex project. Most likely, your thinking pattern will lead you to focus on the technical aspects of the project: data processing, applicability, paying attention to the small details. All these will be highly prioritized by you, and your communication with your employees will be limited to mere technicalities. In addition, you won't consider your employees' opinions as valuable unless they are supported by facts. But this is exactly how you miss out on benefitting from those team members who have different skills, different thinking styles.

"Besides, you surely realize that an AB type manager doesn't indulge in questions such as '*How can I make my employees feel better?*' He's always busy dictating the rhythm, concentrating on how to make work more effective, more efficient. But some of his best employees, in order to connect with the mission and give it their best shot, need a sense of autonomy, expertise and meaning. This kind of manager hardly stands a chance at linking them to the project and getting the best from them. As a result, some of the employees become less efficient and may even be left out. Often, these are the best employees, the ones the organization would hope to retain."

"Moreover," Rona jumped in, "I am sure you remember the article that was published recently under the name '*The Robot-Accountants Are Coming.*'[25] The future of audit is very clear to most of us. Artificial Intelligence based on 'big data' will perform many of the tasks that today's accountants still perform.

"Yes, you showed me that article," I replied. "It feels like no job is safe from the takeover of robots, Artificial Intelligence and big data, especially not in professional services sectors."

"The Boston Consulting Group predicts that one in four jobs will be replaced by either smart software or robots by 2025. As I see it, accounting as we know it today will significantly change. Many current practices of this profession are at a high risk of disappearing. This day may still be in the future, but part of this transformation has already begun.

"But imagine that one of your team members will, one day, be such a robot who will perform all the tasks that were previously reserved for you, the 'engineer-type accountant' who uses his left side of the brain. In this reality, the 21st-century accountant will be the one who, in addition to his high cognitive and professional skills, will be able to offer a value proposition that goes beyond what a computerized system can provide – one with capabilities that are related to the right side of the brain."

"Rona, thinking about the fact that one day, one of my team members may be such a robot, sounds frightening to me. I have to admit that I cannot even imagine such a situation, let alone describe my feelings. What will accounting firms do in order to differentiate themselves and offer a unique value proposition in such a reality?"

"This is exactly connected to our next topic, which is curiosity, creativity and innovation," Peter answered. "Imagine any department where people are not curious and lack creativity. What would their daily routine look like compared to a department in which people were curious, creative and wanted to discover 'new lands' and impact the industry? What kind of value will these two different departments be able to provide to their clients?

"To understand what I am talking about in a more profound way I really recommend you to read an excellent article published by global consulting firm Bain & Company – '*Taking the Measure of Your Innovation Performance*.'[26] The article discusses the fact that almost all successful innovation relies on one essential ingredient that the writers of the article call the 'BothBrain' approach."

"Please note, Michael, that innovation and the discovery of 'new lands' are the most required skills in the 21st century. Now, take for example a methodical and analytical leader who acts according to long-accepted practices and familiar habits and avoids the risk of leaving his comfort zone. How can he lead his employees to any type of innovation? I am not referring to groundbreaking discoveries, but rather to processes within the department that could lead to a significant improvement in the clients' and employees' value proposition."

"I agree," I commented. "Before we left for our journey, Rona told me that our chairman, Mr. John Veihmeyer, concluded in the 2016 CEOs Outlook that *we should all constantly apply innovative approaches to meet our clients' evolving needs, whether they seek advice for targeted change programs or end-to-end support for enterprise-wide transformation.*'

"But notice that by quoting this statement I mean that I do agree that a leader who has innovative ideas must use his engineering skills in order to bring them to life. In the daily work, if an idea is going to be executed and becomes a working method or an innovative service, it must first be assimilated. Many people have good ideas, but a good idea without an action plan is like an abstract science or an unrealized theory."

"Still, Michael," Rona responded, "how can such a methodical and analytic 'engineer-type' leader who acts by the rules and avoids risks lead his employees to innovation?"

"Well said," Peter replied and continued, "Today, it's evident that organizations that do not reinvent themselves are destined to disappear. In addition, most leading managers are AB types. The combination of these two factors has led our economy to the crisis that is being felt by so many."

"Now I start connecting the dots," I admitted. "Last week, Martha introduced us to Professor Richard Florida, who wrote a very interesting book called *'The Rise of the Creative Class'*[27] which provides a fascinating look into the forces reshaping today's and tomorrow's economy. He also tries to deal with the question of how companies, communities and people can survive and prosper in uncertain times. He mainly talks about the growing role of creativity in our economy. Again I have to admit that I thought that whatever he described will indeed happen in the far future."

"This brings me to the last issue I wanted to discuss with you – Passion!" Rona said. "I believe that the main attribute of a passionate accountant today is being a self-directed lifelong learner in the five fields outlined by the 'Whole Advisor' model. Now, think about passion Michael – what does it mean to you?"

"Well, Passion is one of our important characteristics at KPMG," I said.

"And indeed, Martha once gave us a questionnaire in one of our workshops that examined the degree to which each of us had a lifelong learning approach," I suddenly recalled. "I must admit that I was skeptical about the whole matter, especially about the questionnaire. I don't even remember if I actually checked what my results were."

"You're right about the questionnaire," Rona continued. "Martha and I use it quite often. It's a shame you didn't treat it more seriously, because it's very meaningful and serves as a good indicator for the level of passion you have towards your profession and in general, in your daily work and in your relationships with colleagues and clients.

"When I talk about passion, I am referring to the work of global consulting firm Deloitte, which studied the concept of passion.[28] I'm talking about leaders who have a strong emotional connection to their field of expertise and are driven to do their best. They have an intense desire to be thought leaders in their field and wish to have a long-term impact on their field, both locally and globally. They invest their time and energy in places where their impact could be greater and always look for the next thing in the five fields of the 'Whole Advisor' model.

"They have a tendency for exploration, which drives them to go out of their way to find new areas of interest, to break the boundaries of the present, to search for new opportunities in their field and to learn new skills. They are always looking for new challenges, and as a result, they leave their comfort zone on a regular basis. Their creativity and their ability to think outside the box lead them to discover new ways of improving their performance. They focus on the opportunities instead of the obstacles and actively seek challenges in order to reach more advanced stages in their field.

"Also, they look for people with similar interests because they understand that the more they expand their network of contacts, the greater their chance of learning from others. They seek out meaningful relationships with relevant figures in their field of expertise in order to reach new insights, to learn and improve, irrespective of their level of knowledge. Finally, they will do anything to help their employees and clients succeed, and that is where they focus their energy."

"Wow," I said in order to stop this flux of information for a second and internalize it. "I have been listening to you attentively for an hour now, and what you're describing really changes my way of thinking about my profession."

"We've talked about innovation and passion," Peter said, "so let me give you another example to emphasize the importance of developing all four parts of the brain. Suppose you are leading some kind of change process in your department. You go to your team describing the expected change, the circumstances leading to it, its objectives and its implementation plan. You were taught this when you were trained to be a manager at KPMG, and you know how to do it. Only now, in order to keep up with the ever-increasing pace of the changes, you will have to introduce a new round of changes once every few months, instead of once every few years.

"This requires a lot of awareness and willingness to invest time and effort in your employees. One should remember that each of your employees is unique and has a distinct mindset and perception. Each is in a different place in life and troubled by different issues. Each understands you differently and asks different questions. The important thing in leadership is understanding the preferences and positions of others in order to assist individuals in communication and cooperation."

Peter changed the display on the screen, and a second table of Herrmann's appeared.[29] This time, it dealt with change. "Now, let's see what each of the character types might ask about an upcoming change."

"When you speak to an A type, the logical team member, you will surely have to address the issues concerning the bottom line and the facts. As a team member, he will expect to get a full and clear definition of the goals and objectives of the change, as well as detailed information about its financial aspects.

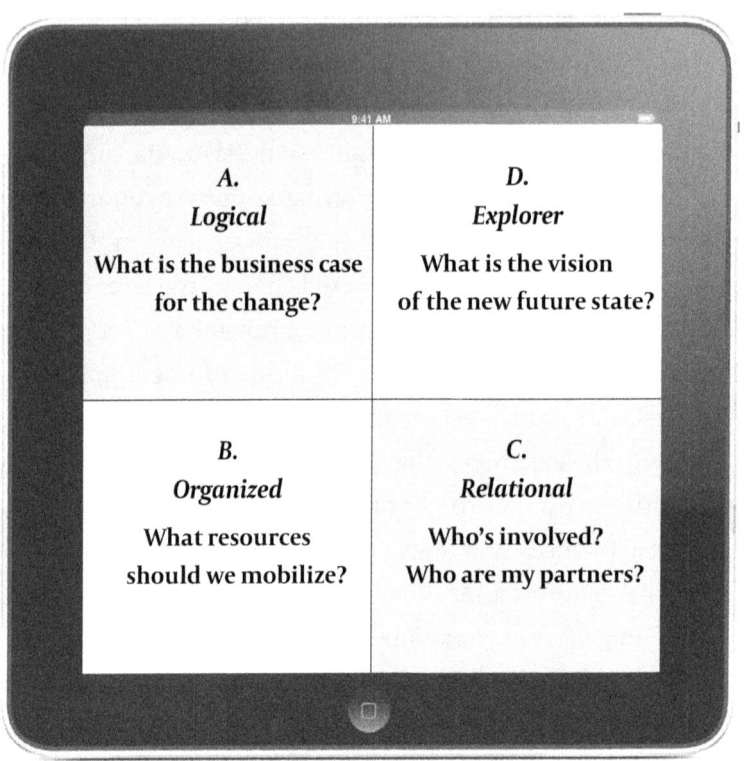

"On the other hand, the B type, the organized team member, will focus on the resources that need to be mobilized to minimize the risk of surprises. For that purpose, he will expect to get relevant references about the specifics of the change – the timeline, known risks, statistics and performance history.

"By now, you can already figure out that a totally different approach will be required in order to meet the concerns of the C type, the relational team member. Above all, he will be concerned with the implications and emotional impact the change will have on him and his family, team members and clients. He will want to know who needs to be involved, who his partners are, and who will be there to listen to concerns.

"Finally, in order to get the D type, the explorer team member, on board, a clear vision of the future state should be communicated. The explorer will frequently ask 'why' questions and expect to have the freedom to influence the process. As he prefers to keep his options open, he will have concerns about constraints or restrictions. He will also need to know how the change may affect his future and how it fits into the overall big picture."

"I see," I said. "But how can a single leader lead such a process so that all his team members are on his side? How can he simultaneously accommodate the different preferences and needs of each employee?"

"Now we've hit the bottom line," Peter said, "and that's why we are really worried here. Our conclusion is that only a 'whole-brained' or 'multi-dominant' executive who is equally capable of using all four parts of the brain, and who is capable of reacting to the whole variety of challenges posed by management, can do it successfully. But studies show that only 2.5% of the population truly show equal strength in all four quadrants."

He looked at me and continued, "Do you see this picture hanging on the wall to the left? We got it from a good friend in Mindset Land. Notice that there is an X mark above four of the ten executives. These marks indicate the 40% of executives who, according to international studies, would not be reappointed to their positions under the current conditions if their candidacy was to be reconsidered."

"Yes, Rona told me about it, but why?" I asked.

"The reason is simple. There are quite a few leaders who are still working according to old principles and are incapable of changing their work habits," Peter answered in a straightforward manner. "Management guru Gary Hamel described it beautifully in one of his lectures in front of a group of our alumni. He sparked objection among most of the business professors when he said that the era of management has ended, and the era of leadership has begun."

"What did he mean?" I asked, feeling that I may have missed something.

"What is the definition of management, Michael?"

"I've never really thought about it," I answered.

"Hamel argues that management is a series of processes that are capable of guaranteeing that a complex system of people and technologies will act in an appropriate manner. The most important aspects of management are planning, budgeting, organizing, manpower, control and troubleshooting."

"This definition sounds right to me, and that's exactly what I do at work every day," I said.

"I see. But according to Gary Hamel, this kind of perception about management is out of date."

"Oh, come on, what do you mean by 'out of date'? An executive won't have to do that stuff anymore?"

"He will most certainly have to, but in a different way. Mostly, he'll have to take one more step and switch from merely being an executive to being a leader," Peter answered.

"OK, we've been talking so much about leadership. Maybe it's time for you to explain what you mean by 'leader' and 'leadership.'"

"Hamel argues that leadership is a series of processes that creates organizations or adapts them to substantially changed circumstances. A leader defines how the future is supposed to look, organizes his employees according to this vision and gives them the inspiration that will enable them to get there, despite all the obstacles.

"You see, Michael, in order to become leaders, executives must work with all four parts of their brain. They must maintain their relevance and lead their organization towards innovation and success."

"And do you have such executives?" I asked.

"To a certain extent, yes, we do. And these are the ones the king was referring to when he spoke about handing over the keys of leadership and responsibility. Some executives have realized that the reality has changed and now take courses, advanced studies and workshops to develop and work on their weaker aspects.

"I think that such executives are the harbingers of the 21st century. They have already realized that they will become irrelevant if they fail to undergo personal change. This is the first time that so many executives fear becoming irrelevant even more than they fear the change itself. This is not trivial, since most of them usually resist change." Peter smiled, "We are talking about AB-type executives who realized that the skills that promoted them up to their current position will no longer work and that they should evolve from being executives to being leaders."

"So, are these the people who are capable of making the switch, training themselves to use all four parts of their brains?"

"Yes, indeed," Peter said, "You had visited Mindset Land before you came here, so you must realize that the individuals capable of making the change are those executives with a growth mindset, those who believe that the brain can evolve and develop through learning. Obviously, an executive with a fixed mindset won't be able to make the necessary change – he wouldn't even know where to begin and would lack the conviction required for success. As a result, he won't be motivated enough to start such a change on his own, and if we force him to, he will most probably fail."

"And what will become of these executives?"

"Executives with a fixed mindset will quickly discover that their value proposition has diminished, and that they have become less desirable. I admit that we all initially tend towards one or two preferred thinking styles, which influence all our skills, relationships and decision-making processes, for better and for worse. But, as I mentioned, we are also sure that these preferences are not rigid and that most people are capable of adopting new and different approaches. It is possible to learn how to expand the variety of our behaviors and act in styles different than the ones we naturally prefer."

He paused for a moment to think and continued, "We might not have a choice and will have to relocate our executives to Mindset Land for a few years. I only hope we have the time to do it. The king fears that if we wait any longer, it will be too late, and his kingdom will cease to prosper. You see, this is the first time in history that we are required to work with all four parts of our brain, and our success, as well as the success of our executives, depends on it!"

The sound of an incoming message interrupted him. "One moment, please," he said, "I just received an interesting e-mail from a colleague of mine in another land, EQ Land. I believe that our answer lies there, but I simply do not have the time for this trip..."

"Isn't that the next land we were going to?" I asked Rona. She smiled and said, "It's definitely the next stop on our journey."

"Couldn't you just come along?" I asked Peter.

"I would really love to, but I have some important and urgent experiments I must conclude," he answered. "Still, I would be more than happy to receive any bit of information you can gather during your visit, if you believe it might help my staff and me make progress. I have no doubt that our king would also value your contribution."

"With pleasure," I answered, feeling sad about the current state of the kingdom.

***

"What will become of our society in the 21st century?" I asked Rona after saying goodbye to Peter.

"Our society will have more and more expert professionals, an abundance of engineers, lawyers, accountants and bankers, for one simple reason: today, far more people go to college, and this trend will only increase. In most professions, there will be no shortage of people with bachelor's, master's or doctoral degrees who have studied in a system that primarily develops the left side of the brain. But today's new reality will present them with challenges that are far more complex than those of the past, those they were used to. Therefore, there will be a strong need for individuals capable of using the four parts of their brain – those who can identify the change, get people together, lead them through a meaningful vision and help the organization to reinvent itself. Today, most executives, no matter how talented, find it difficult to work in a changing work environment, in situations of obscurity and vagueness, without having a clear map of the points of interest that they should reach. These are precisely the executives who are becoming irrelevant."

"But you can't ignore the fact that these executives have succeeded thus far," I said. "And I still know such executives that work at the firm."

"True," Rona said, "but just as the king said, the keys to the kingdom are passing on to new hands. The rules of the game have changed."

"Yes, I do remember your long speech at the start of our journey about being in the midst of a revolution – globalization, economic crises and competition – leading innovation and creativity to become important elements in every organization. You also talked about social responsibility, regulation and rapid technological changes, which all require adaptation."

"That's right," Rona answered, "I also said that the result of all this is that the knowledge experts are no longer capable of providing a full solution and that there is a need for people with the ability to synthesize and innovate."

"OK," I continued, "If I put together everything you've brought up until now, you are referring to the *Artgineer* – the type of person who is both an engineer and an artist. At this point, the importance of partners' and leaders' ability to lead change is clear to me. The importance of their ability to create an emotional bond with their clients and a relationship based on trust is also clear to me. They must also know how to successfully deal with sophisticated clients and provide them with a winning value proposition, how to inspire and keep their most talented employees in the firm and increase their passion, and how to introduce the most advanced technologies in the field into their daily practice."

"Very good," Rona replied. "You have come a long way now, and made all the right connections. Now, let's go further and talk about KPMG's five brand attributes. As mentioned in the last senior partners' convention in Prague, where the senior partners discussed their contribution to our strategy, these attributes actually support our brand promise."

"Are you talking about Expert, Global Mindset, Passionate, Results-driven and Innovative?"

"Yes, this is exactly what I am talking about," Rona replied. "The five brand attributes represent what our current and future clients really expect to get from us. They help us create and deliver a great value proposition and provide our clients with experiences that are unique, distinctive and compelling. Finally, they actually feed into our vision and help us to maintain the KPMG story and bring it to life.[30]

"Now, think about those in the context of leaders who are able to use all four parts of their brain."

"I totally understand the message, Rona. Only leaders and employees who can use all four parts of their brain will be able to manifest these five brand attributes and provide our clients with unique, distinctive and compelling experiences.

"And now, come to think of it – can we also speak of a growth mindset attitude when we talk about an organizational culture?" I asked.

"Yes, we certainly can, and we should do it more often. Professor Dweck took the concept of mindset one step forward and started to talk about a growth and a fixed mindset on an organizational level. She went with her team to seven Fortune 1000 companies and presented the employees and leaders with statements such as, *'When it comes to being successful, this company seems to believe that people have a certain amount of talent.'* The teams had to answer by yes or no. After creating the profile of the company, Professor Dweck and her team tried to find out how the mindset of the company influences important aspects of the organization such as employees' satisfaction, levels of collaboration, innovation, and ethical behavior.

"You should also know, Michael, that when Satya Nadella took over as Microsoft's CEO in 2014, he wanted to shake up the company's culture in order to meet the challenges of the new era we are all facing now. To do so, he chose to cultivate a culture of a growth mindset attitude. Not many people are aware that a growth mindset is the first component of Microsoft's culture, and I am quoting: *'At Microsoft, we're insatiably curious and always learning. We ask questions, take risks and build on each other's ideas, because we are better together. We lean into uncertainty, take risks and move quickly when we make mistakes, because we know that failure happens along the way to innovation and breakthrough.'* You can go to their website and check it, Michael.

"In a new interview with Bloomberg's Dina Bass, Nadella shared that it was the book of professor Carol Dweck that lead him to realize the philosophical core of the change he was trying to create at Microsoft. You can read about it in the article *'How Microsoft Uses a Growth Mindset to Develop Leaders'* which was published in Harvard Business Review."[31]

"Wow," I said, "I can't wait to read the results of their research and more about the process that the CEO of Microsoft led."

"I don't want to spoil the mood but it's also important for me to stress at this point that when it comes to accounting, there are six very powerful killers and enemies of progress and change, as mentioned two years ago by the AICPA in an article with the title *'Becoming the Firm of the Future.'*[32] Among these killers and enemies of progress is the famous comfort zone. In fact, partners and leaders, as most of us, really like things the way they are so they ignore or discount the dramatic changes on the horizon. Another change killer, which sounds very scary to me, is the overconfidence of executive committees in their ability to lead successfully in the white water rapids.

"That brings me to the next enemy of progress, which is vested anchoring. Partners really believe that past successes of their firm will inevitably lead to future ones, which robs them of any motivation to change and go forward. Roy talked about it in our last leadership meeting, if you remember. And the last change killer which I would like to mention is the herding instinct – the fact that many partners prefer to fail as a group than to be perceived as an individual who did something foolish and is unsuccessful, something that we have discussed in Mindset Land."

"But how do we overcome these killers of progress and change and become Artgineers?" I asked. "And who are the leaders that will be able to lead their firms to greatness if so many partners will feel and act in a way that disrupts the process? And, at the same time, these same disruptions will depict those leaders as unsuccessful."

"This is a very good question Michael. I do think that at KPMG, using our Story, we found the best way to deal with it.

If we succeed in being true to all elements of the KPMG Story, employees and clients will find these qualities in each and every one of us. Think about our journey, and remember that every change starts at the mindset level – we must start from the mindset of the leaders in the firm."

"One more thing, Rona. I totally understand the mindset stage, but returning to the KPMG brand attributes, successful leaders are those who are also experts in their own fields, hold a global mindset, are result-driven and innovative, and are passionate about their clients and employees. And I certainly know that all of us, as leaders at KPMG, are committed to leaving the firm in a better state than we found it in. Also, you specifically said that those who will succeed in leading the firm to greatness would be the leaders who use all four parts of their brain. But as we have just heard from Peter, such people are rare. So what's going to happen?"

"Let's continue our journey and find out. Perhaps you will be able to help not only yourself, but an entire land!

"But let me add one more thing, Michael, before we leave. As you already know, our next destination is the EQ Land. Before we arrive, I would like to share with you a few notes from the insightful book of Prof. Klaus Schwab, the Founder and Executive Chairman of the World Economic Forum, *'Shaping the Fourth Industrial Revolution.'*[33] According to Prof. Schwab, Emotional Intelligence is especially needed in the Fourth Industrial Revolution."

"But why now, Rona?" I asked.

"As we all know, Michael, we all operate in a fast-changing reality. Leaders and employees will need to become comfortable with the unknown and remain both hopeful and alert about what comes next. They will need to be creative in how they respond to the complexity of the systems around them and yet remain humble enough to know that they cannot understand it all. I am sure Michael you can make the connections between Prof. Schwab's insights and your role as a future leader. There is nowadays reputable evidence that Emotional Intelligence is one of the biggest predictors of performance in the workplace and a strong driver of leadership. Without a good amount of emotional intelligence, many professionals and leaders will find it difficult to achieve their personal and professional goals."

"And one more last thing, Michael," Rona smiled. "Talking about your firm and the KPMG Story I think that by now you can understand that the people who created this process are brilliant because they found the best way to help people change their mindsets – which is by telling a story. A good story relates to all four parts of the brain and therefore helps more people to change their mindset and make progress. They could have called it our 21st-century strategy or our strategy, but they understood the power of a good story. Maybe one of them read what Peter Drucker said about Strategy and Culture."

"Who is Peter Drucker, and what did he say?" I asked impatiently.

"Mr. Drucker is one of the most influential people in the leadership field. Actually, he is the founder of modern management. He said that '*culture eats strategy for breakfast*.'"

It took me a minute, but I got it – strategy without a healthy culture that is based on a deep set of values and high purpose won't work anymore. And of course, only the leaders who use the whole brain will be able to build a healthy and a winning organizational culture.

4
EQ Land

We arrived at EQ Land as night fell. All I knew about this land was that it was the land of emotional intelligence and that EQ stood for Emotional Quotient, as an analogy to IQ (Intelligence Quotient – the intelligence evaluation scale we are all familiar with).

Although I was exhausted, I couldn't stop thinking about the people with the tilted heads we saw in Artgineer Land. I kept thinking about Peter, devoting all his time and effort to this quest of finding ways to enable individuals to acquire the skills that will help them successfully cope with the challenges of the 21st century. I remembered Peter's request to fill him in on what was happening in EQ Land. Keeping in mind his hopes for what could be learned from this land, I promised myself I would document the knowledge acquired here and send him the highlights.

***

Even though I had slept for 10 straight hours, I woke up tired and moody. Thinking about all the valuable knowledge I had acquired during my journey, I wondered – why did it make me feel confused and even pessimistic, rather than excited and happy? After all, I had already realized that I'd better start making efforts to overcome major gaps with regard to my mindset, the five fields of the '*Whole Advisor*' model and the way I was using the four parts of the brain. It was clear to me that if I wanted to succeed as a future partner, and even more so as a leader, I wouldn't be able to avoid developing my soft skills. I mean my critical skills...

I had already realized that I must put in some real effort to fill in the large gaps in my skills. But why did this understanding bring me down? After all, I have never been deterred by learning new things – on the contrary.

Thinking about it all, I realized that no matter how hard I tried, I would never excel at soft skills and everything that has to do with leadership. As I saw it, I would have to be satisfied with the ambition of reaching an average level, rather than an excellent one. Mostly, I was frustrated by the thought that I will probably have to work hard and invest much time and energy just to achieve mediocre results. I felt like a fish out of water. I just wanted to return home to my comfort zone. I missed my wife Mia, my friends, and mostly, embarrassing as it is to admit, I missed sitting at my computer with the audit accounts and the unfinished reports I had left.

This was my mood as I arrived at the hotel lobby, where I met Rona for morning coffee. She must have sensed my mood, and welcomed me with a pleasant smile and cheerful words. She told me that she thought I had come a long way since the beginning of our journey and that she was really impressed by the basic curiosity and the sensitivity I showed towards the people we met. I thanked her from the bottom of my heart. During the time we spent together, I realized that in spite of her quiet presence, she knew what I was going through and displayed quiet concern. At the beginning of our journey, I was disturbed by the fact that she didn't talk about herself. But now, I felt that she did this out of respect and with the intention of giving me the space I needed in order to grow.

"Michael, you have the morning off," Rona said. "You can go out on your own and take a look around. I thought it would be nice for you to have some time to yourself, after taking guided and educational tours in the two previous lands we visited. Meanwhile, I'll benefit from the fact we're here to visit a friend I haven't seen in years. Go have fun, and I'll meet you for lunch at the national library."

"I understand that you're proposing that I get acquainted with this land on my own, in order to free myself from some fixed mindset I may have?" I asked jokingly.

Rona smiled, "Actually, I hadn't thought about it, but it seems to me that this is indeed the point. You see? You're already living the insights from Mindset Land. So go on, go out and have fun. And don't forget that optimism is a key factor for becoming a successful 21st-century leader. It's also one of the most important life skills."

I left the hotel with my tablet, intending to document life around here and add some of my insights and interpretations. I was eager to understand what the land of emotional intelligence was all about. Going out was good for me, and the cool refreshing air helped me regain my spirits. I walked around for a bit and finally came to a wide and beautifully cultivated park with green lawns, outdoor games, running tracks and fitness equipment. I sat on a vacant bench and watched long-tailed squirrels running along the grass, dogs running free in a designated area, parents playing with their children and a group practicing Tai Chi. The people were pleasant and friendly to one another. Their faces showed that they were content with their lives. Based on their appearance, they didn't seem very wealthy, and so I was surprised by their easygoing spirit, which was so different from the reality I was accustomed to.

I was busy writing down my insights about this advanced leisure culture when a young woman who had just finished jogging sat down beside me. "Good morning," she said smiling.

"My name is Anna, and I guess that you are a tourist, if I may say so."

"Good morning to you too. My name is Michael. And yes, I am a tourist. What gave me away, if I may ask?" I smiled at her, surprised by her direct approach.

"Well, your appearance blends in nicely with the scenery, but your facial expressions give you away," she replied. "No offense, but it's very easy to identify tourists by their facial expressions. It always seems to me that you have only the basic ones: happiness, sadness, fear, surprise, contempt... but you lack the more subtle expressions."

"What do you mean?"

"Here in EQ Land, our nonverbal channels of communication are highly developed. And for this reason, we have many nuances in our body language, a wider variety of movements and facial expressions. Besides, I believe that our basic facial expression, our default expression, is much happier. Tourists who come here always seem less happy to me, compared to us."

"And how do you explain the fact that people feel happier here?"

"Happiness derives from a sense of success in life. At least that's how it is for me."

"Actually, I'm just in the midst of a journey where I'm learning how to become a successful leader. May I ask what success is to you?" I asked the obvious question.

"Oh, that is a subject for long discussions. Did you know that you can find more than 500 definitions for the word or the concept of success? But here in EQ Land, we identify with the definition proposed by the developmental psychologist Howard Gardner, who defined success as one's ability to set goals, make plans, achieve one's objectives and feel satisfied and happy upon achieving them."

"I learned about him in the land I visited earlier, Mindset Land. He also proposed the theory of *Multiple Intelligences*," I remembered.

"True," Anna answered, "I'm surprised you know of him. Not many people outside of EQ Land are familiar with him."

"Interesting," I said, "So, actually, according to his definition, the feeling of happiness is an inseparable part of success..."

"That's right," Anna replied, "and from what I've heard about other places, it appears to me that it's easier to feel success around here. Each of us sets their own objectives according to their personal priorities and whatever makes them feel satisfied and happy. For instance, I have a friend whose objective is to become a CEO and another friend whose objective is to raise her children and spend as much time with them as possible. Both of them invested their time and effort into achieving their objectives and are considered successful."

She looked at me and continued, "Here, if you consciously set a goal for yourself, make a plan and achieve it, you are considered successful."

"But aren't some people more valued than others?" I wondered, "For example people who have accumulated more degrees, more accomplishments or higher income levels?"

"In the past, we too measured success in terms of money and titles. People were considered successful if they spent all day at work and if they accumulated many assets or 'big' bank accounts. Academic degrees were then merely a way to reach prestigious positions. But since then we have moved forward. Today, beyond our professional titles and financial achievements, an important part of our success is related to our personal development. Success criteria now include the extent to which we realize our potential in various aspects of life. It's about how well balanced and comfortable we feel. Beyond nurturing careers, we emphasize emotional, physical, familial and social well-being.

"People who set their objectives and consistently strive to achieve them are considered successful by us, rather than people who let society determine what success is for them. If you fail to make up your own definition of success, how can you know where to look for it? How can you identify it when it comes, and how can you enjoy its fruits?

"Harvard Medical School has been running the longest

research on happiness, well-being and success in modern history[34] For over 75 years, Harvard's Grant and Glueck study tracked the physical and emotional well-being of two populations: 456 poor people in Boston and 268 graduates from Harvard's classes of 1939–1944. The clearest and most surprising message of this impressive study, according to Robert Waldinger,[35] the director of the Harvard Study of Adult Development, is that good relationships keep us happier and healthier, not money, status or position. For many people outside EQ_Land, this is a big surprise, but not for us. Most people in various countries don't really understand it and don't invest enough in their relationships. And in the end, they find themselves very lonely and very unhappy. I even read last week that Theresa May, Prime Minister of the United Kingdom, has appointed one of her ministers to lead on issues connected to loneliness.[36] A minister of loneliness, can you imagine?"

"So, you're saying that the majority of people here invest in other areas beyond their careers. What does it say about ambition and being competitive? Are those left aside?" I asked.

"People here are most certainly ambitious, but their priorities are apparently different from yours," Anna answered. "We strive for fulfillment and success in a variety of areas, in addition to our professional lives. Our ambition is expressed in the fact that we strive for full and satisfying personal lives, for our families, our friends and for ourselves. We make sure to maintain our health and emotional well-being."

"Is it possible for everyone to succeed?" I asked. "After all, isn't it normally the case that the success of some comes at the expense of others?"

"Once again, it all depends on how you perceive success. If you measure, examine and compare yourself to others, you have a problem. Here, we have figured out that one's success doesn't come at the expense of others because success is determined according to personal criteria. We are all different people, with different strengths and different objectives, busy fulfilling different roles, which require different skills.

"For this reason, everyone can succeed if they perform well. We understand that we only compete against ourselves. That is the reason that each of us makes our best effort to improve and strengthen personal abilities. Of course, it doesn't mean that we expect to succeed at any given moment. We would most certainly grasp a lack of success as a temporary situation that will pass."

"I get the impression that you have some knowledge and capabilities that I lack," I said. "You say that you live a full and fulfilling life here. What's the secret to your success? And how do I learn it?"

"We have neither a secret nor a magic spell. Our sense of self-worth in life derives from our recognition of the world of values and emotions and the benefit we get from nurturing it. Emotions are a language, and our parents teach us this language from the moment we are born. They display a full range of emotions, and that's how we learn the nuances and acquire the legitimacy to use these emotions in order to express ourselves. Our kindergartens and schools also emphasize the emotional world – we develop our children's 'muscles of Emotional Intelligence' or 'muscles of success,' as we often refer to them. These muscles connect emotion and reason or, you could also say – the abilities of the left-brain and the right-brain.

"Practicing and flexing our emotional intelligence 'muscles' enable us to process our feelings and weigh the impact of emotion and intuition within our thinking and decision-making process. This practice of weighing our emotions as part of rational processes is also what gives us a fuller life experience. People here learn to live with a high level of self-awareness while controlling their impulses. They practice life skills such as persistence and perseverance, and they enhance their social compatibility skills."

"I must ask you something, and I hope you don't take it the wrong way," I hesitated. "We know about a trade-off, an exchange or a compromise, occurring in nature when certain abilities are developed at the expense of others. I find it interesting – is it possible that one would develop higher emotional intelligence at the expense of other skills, or vice versa? I personally can attest, for instance, that my logical-technical tendency is more developed, at the expense of my interpersonal skills. Many of my friends from the university and my work colleagues are similar in this sense. How is this manifested here?"

Anna smiled, "Is it just me or are you implying that emotional intelligence is a nice consolation prize, at the expense of IQ? Are these two qualities interchangeable, and do we really have to compromise? Let me tell you, and I have no intention of insulting of course, that this approach belongs to an old and dogmatic school of thought. I wouldn't argue with an example of an animal that can see better than it hears, or vice versa. But as far as human beings are concerned, you must set aside these theories, or else you will remain limited in both your thinking and your life skills.

"Just as I do, you probably also know some highly intelligent individuals who are also emotionally developed, as well as others who lack both IQ and EQ. Plus, there are many in-between cases.

"Each of us can develop and refine our abilities, beginning from our own starting point. If you exercise and build your emotional intelligence muscles, you can strengthen the links between the various parts of the brain and increase the flexibility of your thinking. The connection between emotion and reason is very central – the rational refines the emotional while the emotional feeds and informs the rational. Try to remember how many times you've had a gut feeling about a particular individual even before anything was said. This gut feeling is a signal from your emotional mind, and only later does the rational mind come in..."

I had many other questions to ask Anna, but a quick look at my watch revealed that it was already lunchtime, and I was late to meet Rona.

I thanked Anna for the valuable insights she shared with me. "I thank you for the pleasant conversation as well," she replied. "And please excuse me if I was too preachy. I just feel that we've reached a formula for a healthy and balanced life, and I want to share these simple insights with anyone who wants to listen."

***

As I was leaving the park and pondering over what Anna had said, I accidentally took the wrong bus and arrived at another part of the city. It took me 15 minutes to realize my mistake. When I finally asked a group of people how to get to the national library, I was treated kindly, and they showed a great willingness to help. One of them even insisted on escorting me to my bus stop to avoid mistakes.

The bus ride took about half an hour, and eventually the driver stopped at the entrance to a large building. "This is the national library," the driver pointed toward the building. I wondered why, of all places in EQ Land, Rona had chosen to meet with me at the library.

As I entered the large building, I realized that we had never specified any meeting place. Based on my acquaintance with Rona and the experience of our journey together, I went up to the floor where they had books about personal growth and psychology, but she wasn't there. The familiar scent of her perfume revealed her location, sitting next to the shelves under a large sign: **Success in the 21st Century.**

I approached her and apologized for being late. Rona invited me to take a seat and asked, "Have you ever asked yourself how come there are so many books, and yet people never stop writing and adding knowledge on any given topic?"

"Honestly, I never thought about it," I replied.

"I believe that the reason for this is that we still have many questions with insufficient answers," Rona said. "Each time I enter a library or a large bookstore I think about all the concepts, questions, doubts, creativity and passion for discovery that accompanies and motivates writers while writing a book."

I nodded, and Rona continued. "For instance, take the concept of success. People have been coping with the question of the essence of success for a very long time now. There are many books written on this topic, yet people still find it difficult to define success. But you know that ever since I was exposed to the concept of emotional intelligence, the word that immediately comes to mind in this context is *success*."

I told her about my meeting with Anna and about the definition she provided for the concept of success, the one borrowed from Gardner.

"Yes, exactly," Rona answered. "I also think that Gardner was able to define success in a simple and precise manner. And now, I want to ask you some questions through which we'll be able to learn about the valuable insights of emotional intelligence and the road to success in a changing world."

"What kind of questions?" I asked curiously.

"First, who is the person that influenced your life the most? And second, what was special about this person?"

I wasn't prepared for this kind of question. Since I already knew Rona well enough to know that she wouldn't settle for a superficial answer, I asked for a few minutes to organize my thoughts. Many people were and still are significant in my life, and all of them crossed my mind: friends, army officers, teachers and family members. I had met so many fine individuals throughout my life, people who believed in me, helped me make important decisions and served as an inspiration. But the more I thought about it, the clearer it was to me which one of them I would like to mention: Jacob, my great-uncle, who passed away years ago. He had been by my side since I was a young boy, when I emigrated with my parents from Argentina to Israel. Without any doubt, he was the most extraordinary individual I had ever known, and his character greatly influenced my life.

I started talking rapidly, "The person who influenced me the most was Jacob, my grandfather's brother. He was a daring person who was never afraid to do the things he believed in. From a very young age, he figured out that Israel was the best place for him to start a family and decided to emigrate. He never waited for others to make up their minds for him, and that was the case this time as well. He always made courageous and complex decisions. He was an independent pioneer who knew what he had to do to get what he wanted.

"He told me that when he first applied for immigration assistance from the Jewish Agency, his application was turned down because his wife suffered from a severe lung disease. But he never gave up and was determined to achieve his goal. He wrote letters to officials at the highest levels saying that he wouldn't give up and that he believed that in Israel, his wife would be able to live for many years in spite of her illness. Eventually, he was successful, and she did, in fact, enjoy a long and full life in Israel.

"He was one of the most determined and positive people I have ever met. He could always 'see the glass half full' and enjoy the positive aspects of each moment. He also had a talent for making everyone around him see the positive side of things, just as he did. He had a kind heart. I remember many people seeking his help, and he helped each and every one of them. I remember how much he helped my family when we immigrated. Apart from him, we really had no one. He always told me that it was our job to help one another and to contribute as much as possible to the well-being of others. People really loved him, and everyone wanted to be his friend. I think it had to do with his amazing ability to listen. He was a very patient listener, and he knew how to analyze a situation and help the individual reach a solution.

"And despite all that he did, he always found time to listen to himself as well. He taught me that we should spend a few minutes every morning in contemplation, to think about our situation and how we feel about it, whether we were happy or sad. We should think about what we had to do to be happier. He was definitely one of the most amazing people I have ever met. Many times throughout my life, I stop and think what he would have done or what decisions he would have made in my place. One of the most difficult moments in my life was saying goodbye to him when he died.

"I know how important it was for him to realize his own potential and attain success so he could support himself and his family, while still learning a profession, in a new language, in a new country. He made great efforts, working and going to the university by day and improving his Hebrew reading and writing skills by night."

I suddenly noticed that our library section had nearly emptied while I was speaking. It seems that my enthusiastic tone made people search for a quieter place. I felt slightly embarrassed, but it didn't spoil the positive feeling I was filled with as I remembered Jacob.

Rona smiled and said, "What an interesting story. I bet your grandfather's brother was a very special person who brought much happiness and security to the lives of his family members. You told me he went to university. What did he study?"

"He studied medicine. He always wanted to become a doctor, but he couldn't achieve this in his homeland. When he came to Israel, he knew he couldn't begin his studies right away due to difficulties of language and lack of financial support. But he studied Hebrew, and in a short time, he knew enough to be accepted into medical school. He also worked hard and managed to save enough money to pay for it.

"When I immigrated with my parents and encountered language difficulties, he talked to me about the time he attended medical school. It was one of the most challenging times of his life, under constant pressure from demanding studies, work and family. But Jacob, as always, was able to remain optimistic and was grateful for the opportunities he received. Ever since, whenever I felt challenged, I would go to him and he would tell me about the hard times he went through during his studies and how he was determined to succeed and make it to the finish line."

I continued my story, as the memories flooded back to me. "After his graduation, he started working at Rothschild Hospital in Haifa. He was a devoted and compassionate doctor. He was the kind of doctor who would look his patients in the eye, listen to them and do his best to help them – not only on the physical level but on the emotional and mental levels too. His patients felt that he was there for them, holding their hand and supporting them through tough times. Unfortunately, this is very different from what happens in most hospitals today, where doctors only have several minutes to allocate for each patient. I remember how important it was for him to get to know his patients. He understood the connection between mind and body long before it became trendy. He always said that one of the primary roles of hospital doctors was to calm and soothe patients, as well as reassure their relatives."

"While other doctors rested or chatted during breaks, he would go over to his patients and their families, asking questions, telling stories, joking around with them and helping them relax. When I visited him at the hospital, I saw the broad smiles on the faces of his patients as he entered the room. And, by the way, when he retired, he let us all know that he wasn't the 'stay-at-home' type of guy, and he volunteered as much as he could. It always was important to him that his life would consist of significant acts."

Rona listened and smiled. "Do you remember that I talked about emotional intelligence in our first meeting?" she asked. "You hinted that you suspect that emotional intelligence is designed to support people who could not find a more dignified job."

I nodded and blushed.

"Your great-uncle is a model of an individual and a doctor with high emotional intelligence. I wonder how he developed these abilities. Each sentence about his life was an expression of high emotional intelligence."

"Honestly, Rona, I still don't understand why you sanctify the link between emotion and intelligence. I was taught that one shouldn't mix emotions with decisions in one's business, work or life in general, especially when it comes to making difficult decisions. Throughout my accounting studies it was clearly conveyed that what's important is our ability to analyze, to go into detail and to make decisions. Other than that, I find it hard to believe that one can actually develop skills that are related to emotional aspects."

"With such an attitude, Michael, you may have a pretty good chance of being accepted as a resident of the dreary side of Mindset Land," Rona said with a smile.

"But before we continue, I'd like to challenge you with another question. I would like to hear from you about a book that influenced your life, a book that changed your thinking and led you to significant insights."

I once again took my time and thought about it. In recent years, with all the pressure at work, I mainly read professional literature. The two books that came to mind were *Jonathan Livingston Seagull* by Richard Bach and *The Alchemist* by Paulo Coelho. Both of them were gifts from Mia, but honestly, I didn't really connect to either of them at the time. I was going to answer that I couldn't think of a book that influenced me, but then I remembered Dan, my officer in the army. He was so impressed with the book *'Who Moved My Cheese?'* by Spencer Johnson,[37] that he bought me a copy.

"Would it be all right if I talked about a book that impressed someone else who was very close to me?"

"Sure," Rona answered with a smile.

"Dan was one of the most impressive officers I met during my military service," I opened my story, "an extremely confident guy, full of resourcefulness and determination. He wasn't the type to get good grades at school, but it was clear to everyone that he had what it takes to succeed. Even though he grew up in a poor family, he was sure of his ability to succeed. Every time he heard someone complaining, he would tell them to stop complaining and see what they could do to improve the situation. Dan had the custom of reading at any given moment. There were always several books in his room. One evening, as I walked into his room, I saw him reading a book with the funny name, *Who Moved My Cheese?*"

"I jokingly asked him what happened and if everything was all right. He just said – 'Michael, you have to read this book. It's as if someone took everything I think and believe in, and put it into one book.' When we returned to the base after a week off, he came up to me and said with a smile, 'I believe that if something good happens to you, you have to share it with someone else. I bought you a copy of the book.' I was impressed with the friendly gesture but had no desire to read the book. When I finally read it, the book's messages seemed highly simplistic to me.

"Dan's enthusiasm about the book was so great that he prepared a presentation about it. One evening, he invited all of us to his room and told us the story." I imagined Rona was familiar with the book, but I briefly described it anyway.

"The four protagonists are two 'littlepeople' called *Hem* and *Haw*, and two mice, *Sniff* and *Scurry*. They all live in a maze, in which they look for cheese. The cheese symbolizes all the good things we want in life, happiness and success. After finding a large stock, they enjoy the abundance and establish a daily routine. But one day, they see that there is no more cheese. Both groups, the 'littlepeople' and the mice, represent different approaches to coping with this change.

"The two mice aren't biased with prior beliefs or expectations. Actually, noticing that the cheese supply is diminishing, they have mentally prepared themselves for the task of looking for new cheese. They don't panic but regard the situation as a simple problem. They tell themselves that if the reality has changed, they need to change their course of action as well. So they set out to search for new cheese, which they eventually find.

"In contrast, the two little people, Hem and Haw, go through a deep crisis. They were both caught unprepared since they expected the cheese supply to be constant. One gets angry and wants everything to be back to the way it was before. The other complains and refuses to go looking for new cheese, as he fears the unknown. The two of them just blame each other, waiting for the cheese to return. Eventually, it takes a long time for Haw to realize that he needs to brush aside his fears and return to the maze. He finds new cheese and leaves messages for Hem. Uncompromising, Hem stays behind, stuck in his expectation for the old cheese to return.

"Dan discussed the messages of the story, about how it was important that we stop and evaluate our situation before the cheese disappears. Our fixations might prevent us from finding new cheese, so we should develop our self-awareness and figure out what is holding us back. We should always remember that he who won't change and adapt, will fail. If we want to find new cheese, it's important that we continually move forward, visualize ourselves finding the cheese and enjoying it. If I'm not mistaken, it's called guided affective imagery. In other words, the faster we let go of the old cheese, the sooner we find the new one.

"To be honest, I now see the connection between the things I heard from him 15 years ago and the issues we're dealing with on this journey."

Rona listened intently, and I noticed that she was also taking notes. Eventually, she said, "You've provided us with an excellent example. Your story provided a lot of material about emotional intelligence."

She continued, "I want to tell you about psychologist Dr. Reuven Bar-On. He said that of all he has learned about people over the years, three questions interest him the most.

"The first one is – why are there people with an extremely high IQ who have not achieved much in their professional lives and are not content with their personal lives and relationships? The second question, complementary to the first one, is – how is it that there are people with an average IQ who achieve a great deal in life, enjoy good relationships, have many friends and professional accomplishments, lead teams and organizations, and progress and earn well? And the last question, which I also find intriguing, is – why do some of us enjoy better emotional well-being, happiness and optimism than others?

"Bar-On reached the conclusion that there are several groups of emotional, social and interpersonal competencies, which help us to cope optimally with challenges. They also help us to identify beneficial situations and take advantage of such opportunities. In other words, these are competencies that have behavioral manifestations related to the connection between emotion and cognition, between interpersonal and professional skills. Bar-On actually coined the term EQ as an analogy to IQ.[38]

"Prior to Bar-On, John Mayer and Peter Salovey dealt with the correlation between cognition and emotion and with the definition of emotional intelligence as a form of intelligence.[39] Daniel Goleman also studied the contribution of emotional intelligence abilities to management and leadership. Goleman contributed significantly to the concept by bringing it to the general public in a book that became a best-seller, reached a greater audience and gained popularity."

"What is its title?"

"It has an interesting title: *Emotional Intelligence: Why it Can Matter More than IQ...* "[40] Rona said.

"However, Michael," She continued, "it's important for you to know that there are quite a few researchers who are critical of this research field and the claimed role of emotional intelligence. One of them is Professor Zeidner[41,42] from the University of Haifa. However, even he agrees that emotional intelligence has become one of the most prominent research fields in modern psychology."

"And what you're saying is that emotional intelligence is important for our success as advisors and leaders in a changing and dynamic world?" I asked.

"I believe that emotional intelligence is an essential set of abilities for any advisor, as well as Lawyers, Bankers, Physicians, or even Engineers" Rona replied. "But when it comes to leaders, it is, in fact, one of the most critical components of exceptional leadership."

"What is emotional intelligence composed of?"

"There are several theories, but I would like us to focus on the model that we use in our workshops and change management processes. We created a model made up of ten subscales, which are grouped in four composite scales. Let's take a look at the tablet."

Emotional Awareness & Management	• Emotional Self-Awareness and Expression • Self-Regard • Self-Regulation and Management
Social Skills	• Interpersonal Relationships • Empathy
Adaptability	• Reality Testing and Problem Solving • Flexibility • Stress and Uncertainty Management
Self-Actualization	• Determination • Passion and Influence

"Interesting, but how is it related to the books we talked about, or to Jacob?"

"I will soon show you that the way you described your great-uncle Jacob meets the definition of emotional intelligence. But before that, let's get familiar with the emotional intelligence subscales."

Emotional Awareness & Management

Emotional Self-Awareness and Expression

Emotional Self-Awareness is our ability to attend to emotional information, identify, understand and define our emotions. It is the ability to figure out what causes specific emotions and how they impact our behaviors and others around us. This component also includes the ability to express our emotions openly and authentically. Doing so is important as we can benefit from people's feedback, which helps us better understand our own emotions.

Self-Regard

Self-Regard is our ability to adequately assess our strengths and areas of challenge, to evaluate our possibilities and eventually to accept ourselves fully, to feel able and confident. It is also our ability to acknowledge our successes and achievements and not to over-criticize ourselves.

Self-Regulation and Management

Self-Regulation and Management is our ability to manage our emotions, to persevere and stay on task, control impulses and drives and delay gratification, even in the face of adversity. It is also our ability to deeply reflect and consider matters, without being impulsive or aggressive.

Social Skills

Interpersonal Relationships

The Interpersonal Relationships component is the ability to initiate and maintain positive, reciprocal and mutually satisfying interactions and relationships with others. It is the ability to create a positive atmosphere, be social, show genuine interest in others, build long-lasting relationships and cooperate with others.

Empathy

Empathy is our ability to be attentive and sensitive to the emotions of others. It is our ability to identify and understand how others feel and think, and respond accordingly. In its essence, it is the ability "to walk in others' shoes" and see things from their point of view (without losing our own).

Adaptability

Reality Testing and Problem Solving

In its essence, this component is the ability to understand how emotions impact our perception and our decision making. Reality Testing is the ability to remain objective by seeing things as they really are (and not as we would like or hope them to be). It is the ability to correctly and objectively read situations, to be realistic and practical, to identify challenges and opportunities. Problem Solving is the ability to identify problems on time and to appropriately solve them methodically. Together, Reality Testing and Problem Solving are the main ingredients of creativity and innovation and are crucial to our ability to identify and adapt to changes in a dynamic reality.

Flexibility

Flexibility is our ability to adapt our emotions, thoughts and behaviors to changing conditions, to unfamiliar, unpredictable, and dynamic circumstances or ideas. It is the ability to think creatively and change our minds, when necessary, and therefore to tolerate, embrace, initiate and even lead change.

Stress and Uncertainty Management
This component is the ability to work effectively under stress and uncertainty, to remain calm as well as being able to calm others. It is our ability to constructively manage our emotions, to withstand adverse events, uncertainty and stressful situations by actively and confidently coping with disruptive feelings.
Self-Actualization
Determination
Determination is our ability to stand for our values and beliefs, to express them clearly and respectfully without offending others, and strive to achieve them. It is the ability to persist and work hard, for long periods of time, towards achieving goals.
Passion and Influence
Passion and Influence is the drive to be meaningful and make a lasting impact, to continually search for new areas, break boundaries and seize opportunities for personal as well as team learning and development.

"Rona," I said, after going over the table twice, "I understand why subscales such as stress management and problem solving are essential to my success as a future partner, or as a leader in general. I can even understand, after undergoing such a significant part of our journey, why the interpersonal aspect is important. But it's still unclear to me why subscales such as emotional self-awareness and passion are important to my success as a leader in a high-performance culture."

"That's an excellent question, Michael. Let's talk about the concept of emotional self-awareness and examine its connection to management. Leaders who are highly aware of their emotions understand how they feel in various situations at work. They also know how to use their emotions in order to motivate themselves and others. This helps them in many respects and enables them to understand how others feel and what can be done to assist them. It allows them to realize when they are on the edge, to stop and step back from the situation before they erupt. Also, it allows them to know when they are exhausted and it is time to recharge, and so on.

"Larry Bossidy and Ram Charan wrote the excellent book called *'Execution: The Discipline of Getting Things Done,'* which emphasizes the importance of emotional self-awareness in executive roles.[43] Take a look at the following summary:

- Know thyself… It's the core of authenticity. When you know yourself, you are comfortable with your strengths and not crippled by your shortcomings.
- Self-awareness gives you the capacity to learn from your mistakes as well as your successes. It enables you to keep on growing.
- In no area is emotional self-awareness more important than in the performance culture, which draws on every part of the brain and every aspect of being human.
- If you know yourself, you can control yourself. You can curb your ego, be responsible for your own behavior, adapt to changes, adopt new ideas and stick to your standards of integrity and decency in any given situation.
- Also, self-control is the key to real self-confidence. It is a positive kind of control, rather than other forms of self-control that result from weaknesses or insecurities, such as the intentional display of self-confidence or arrogance."

"I see," I replied after giving it some thought, "you have linked self-awareness, self-control and self-confidence. Now, what can you say about passion?"

"Remember your conversation with Anna, who told you how people are influenced by other people's emotions. Studies show that the first emotion that affects us at work is the emotion of our direct manager. Leaders who feel self-actualized, determined and passionate, make their teams feel energetic, open and excited about their activities. However, if the partner is worn out, feeling bad and unfulfilled, his team will feel the same way: a team without energy, which feels like something is weighing on them and finds everything difficult to accomplish. Passion is the fuel that drives all of us. Can you visualize what these two teams look like?"

"Yes, of course," I answered, "I have a vivid picture of both..."

"After familiarizing ourselves with the various EQ subscales, let's return to Jacob, your grandfather's brother. I want to show you that your description of him fits the definitions of emotional intelligence perfectly. I have taken notes on the things you said, and now we can examine a few examples and analyze them together, using what we have learned about EQ and its subscales.

- You said he never waited for others to make up their minds for him, but always made courageous and complex decisions. These are reality testing, self-regard and determination.
- You said he was one of the most positive people you knew, and that he could always see the glass half full and see the good in any given situation. Here we can see again the subscales of self-regard and determination.

- You mentioned he had a kind heart, that he helped all who approached him, and that he always said it was our duty to help and assist others as much as possible and to contribute to their well-being. Surely you can identify here empathy and interpersonal relationships.
- You also said that people really loved him, that everyone wanted to be his friend, and that you think it was due to his tremendous ability to listen. This is yet another example of his empathy and interpersonal skills.
- You mentioned that he always said that we have to take a few minutes every morning to contemplate our feelings and think about what we should do in order to be more fulfilled. It is evident that he possessed emotional self-awareness.
- He also told you about one of the most challenging periods in his life and said it wasn't easy to live for a long period of time under the stresses of studies, work and family. Namely, he possessed the ability to manage stress and uncertainty, flexibility and self-actualization.

We could go on and on, Michael. It turns out that your grandfather's brother was a human being and a doctor with high emotional intelligence."

"Yes, this is clear to me now. I admit that until now I saw emotional intelligence as something like self-assessment questionnaires in the back of women's magazines. But now, I begin to understand what it is and its connection to success."

"Now let's try to analyze the book that Dan was so excited about."

"You know, I met him about a year ago when I was on reserve duty. We talked all night long. He told me how happy he was with his life and claimed that he had already achieved most of the objectives that he had set for himself during his military service. It is incredible, but even though it has been 15 years, he still talks in terms of the concepts of the book, and I was really happy for him."

"Do you see a parallel between the message of the book and the insights that we're collecting during our journey?"

"Yes," I admitted. "For instance, understanding that change frequently occurs and that we should accept it, adapt very quickly and move on. If I may use the words of Stephen Hasty, the Global Transformation Leader at KPMG – '*Change has become the new normal. The world is moving so quickly today that there really is no steady state*'. He also states that '*CEOs have to be prepared to be in a continual transformation and the ability to change affects results*'. This surely applies to all of us."

"That's true," Rona confirmed. "And moving on is what enables growth, which is critical for leaders and employees. When a sudden change occurs, some of them will be able to adapt to it, while others will fail to adapt and remain stuck where they are. As you can understand by now, changes are taking place and will continue to take place in all fields: management, strategy, competition, customers, employees, technology, regulations and economics."

"But how do you link between the ability to adapt to changes and the abilities related to emotional intelligence?"

"It's very simple, Michael. The capabilities that are listed in the Adaptability composite scale of Emotional Intelligence – such as flexibility, uncertainty management and reality testing – are especially necessary in times of change."

"Now, tell me one more thing," I asked, "Is emotional

intelligence measurable? Do I have any way of knowing where I stand in each of the subscales?"

"Yes, there are several measurable models, the most prominent ones being Mayer and Salovey's MSCEIT, Bar-On's EQ-i and Daniel Goleman's ECI. Bar-On's EQ-i,[44] for example, is a self-report test in which you rate yourself through 133 statements."

"Wow! I didn't know this kind of discipline is measurable. Can I actually see where I am today, in terms of each subscale?"

"Yes, definitely. For each subscale, you will get a numerical score, much like intelligence IQ tests. Below a certain level, a low result will indicate that this subscale is an area of growth for you and that you could benefit from developing it. Your strengths will be the subscales for which you get a high score."

"That sounds fascinating," I said, feeling that I would really like to try it out.

"But you should also notice a significant difference from IQ results. EQ results that are too high come with a price: they mean that you are over-using a certain 'muscle.' For instance, if a leader receives a very high score on the assertiveness subscale, it doesn't necessarily mean that he is highly assertive, but rather that he might be aggressive. Similarly, someone who gets a very high score on the empathy subscale might find it difficult, as a leader, to tell his employees things that could hurt their feelings. Even during feedback conversations, he might find it difficult to tell them where they should improve.

"Now, recall your last conversation with John, as well as your conversation with Martha. Can you try to analyze them according to the EQ subscales?"

"I'll try," I answered. "John claimed that I am insufficiently open to changes and that I tend to postpone or even oppose them in every possible way. He also claimed that I tend to rearrange reality according to my needs, failing to realize the fact that we now operate in a completely new, different and complex reality. It must have adversely influenced my ability to effectively solve problems. In terms of EQ, he must have been talking about my adaptability skills. I certainly wanted to stay in my comfort zoon.

"With Martha, the issue of my interpersonal skills came up – my inability to listen to others, to try and enter their minds and genuinely understand how they feel. I must have been really focused on the professional side and failed to pay attention to where my employees were at. She also told me that clients might get the impression that I didn't really care about them or that I wasn't attentive to their needs. That has to do with interpersonal skills.

"You know," I added, "now that I'm analyzing it with you, I'm starting to realize that I was quite disconnected from the people around me. I didn't give much consideration to the fact that others were influenced by my behavior. I now realize that there are two gauges I never paid attention to – the internal gauge of emotional self-awareness and the external gauge of reality testing."

"Great," Rona said with a smile, "it's incredible how much you've managed to learn and internalize during our journey. Plus, you have begun to realize the importance that this knowledge has for you personally, as a leader and as a human being.

"Some people think that the concept of emotional

intelligence was merely a short-lived, late 20th century trend. However, it is important for you to know that it is as significant as it was during the 20th century. In fact, in the 21st century, emotional intelligence has become utterly critical.

"For a start, don't forget Generation Y, which now constitutes a significant portion of the workforce. You know that this generation is far more committed to its direct managers on a personal basis than it is to the overall organization. Meaning, the interpersonal aspect is critical for leading such people.

"Second, we have described the current work and business environments in terms of gushing white waters, a period in which change is the defining characteristic. And this is why adaptability becomes a key issue. In this ever-changing reality, the ability to work under stressful conditions, over long periods of time, will be required of everyone. That makes the ability to manage stress and uncertainty an essential component of our adaptability! If you are having trouble to cope while rafting in those white waters, it will be very difficult for you to help others stay on board and lead them through challenges.

"Another significant subscale of emotional intelligence is determination. How can heads of markets, and other partners or directors, reinvent themselves and succeed in a highly competitive world without high levels of determination?

"And, last but not least, don't forget our internal source of energy, our fuel, which is our passion. How can we keep on rafting without fuel? The Leaders who will succeed over time are those who will be able to take care of themselves and maintain their feelings of fulfillment."

"But Rona, it seems to me that we are once again neglecting the professional competencies that I acquired for so many years. Are they meaningless?"

"Of course not. Professional competencies are important and even crucial. After all, you can't practice accounting without them. But today, they're simply not enough on their own. Do you remember I told you that I foresee a shortage of competent leaders? As I said, there will be an abundance of professionals and leaders equipped with diplomas, professional skills and experience. However, there is already a shortage of competent professionals who have what it takes to become leaders, to successfully manage themselves and their teams in such a challenging reality, over time.

"I meet a lot of talented professionals and leaders like yourself who feel cheated because, throughout their life, they developed their professional skills rather than their critical skills. And suddenly now, in the new world that has developed, they don't have what it takes to be promoted to managerial positions, if that's what they want. Many of them respond like Hem and Haw: they have yet to internalize that something has changed and still think that success and ability are measured the same way they were a decade ago. They still believe that being strong on the professional side is good enough."

Rona's final statement took me back to my last conversation with John, who tried to make me realize that things were in fact changing. I felt embarrassed as I realized that I had been in complete denial, just like Hem and Haw.

"Rona," I said, "I recall our values at KPMG that create a sense of shared identity and define what we stand for and how we do things – working together, respecting the individual, being open and honest in our communication and of course, leading by example. I can now see that no low EQ leader will be able to act according to these values."

"You are very right Michael. In order to live by our values we need to have leaders and employees with high EQ. Moreover, we must have such leaders and employees in order to live and fulfill our purpose – to 'Inspire Confidence and Empower Change' and to achieve our vision of becoming the Clear Choice of our clients. I cannot imagine any low EQ leader who is able to create an organizational culture in which employees are caring, passionate and share a lasting pride in their firm. In addition, we do differentiate ourselves from other firms, and we want our clients to see the difference in us. I cannot imagine a leader without emotional intelligence bringing that about.

"And one more thing Michael," Rona added, "talking about EQ and our unique value proposition, I want you to know that in the UK CEO Outlook of 2017, research has identified three distinct CEO character types - the 'Positive Disruptor', the 'High EQ CEO' and the 'Investor CEO'. Of course, many will identify with a blend of these. Being a 'High EQ CEO' is less about revenues and leading from the front, but more about bringing teams together and acting as a catalyst to achieve better, faster results."[45]

"So, how do we develop emotional intelligence?"

"The good news is, as I mentioned before, that we can develop all the components of emotional intelligence. But there are two critical conditions for that. The first is to have a growth mindset. The second is to internalize that it's going to be a long process that requires investment and may be painful. Unfortunately, you can't go through it under full anesthesia and wake up after the procedure is over, with the doctor saying 'the operation was a success, and you are free to go,' like some would like it to be.

"And we also have to overcome the six change killers that we spoke of in Artgineer Land. We need to create a real sense of urgency in the firm, mainly among the partners and the directors. As I see it, the firms' senior partners must do it themselves. I don't think that they can delegate this important task to anyone else in their firms."

"Well, this is exactly what Roy told us in our last meeting," I said. "And I understand now that we are talking about a long process. Knowing Roy, I am sure that he has a good plan for creating that sense of urgency."

"Now, Michael, I'd like to make a strong connection between the three lands we have visited up to now, and I will do it by following an article I truly enjoyed,[46] titled 'Increase Your Return on Failure.' The writers believe that the new reality we are all facing now has changed the definition of what it means to 'be smart.' Up to now, many leaders achieved success by being 'smarter' than other employees, as measured by grades and test scores. The smart people of the 20th century were those who received the highest scores by making the fewest mistakes. Of course, this means a fixed mindset attitude or culture.

"As opposed to this 'Old Smart,' the 'New Smart' is the person who can promote higher levels of cognition or human thinking and emotional engagement. The new smart is the Artgineer. The 'New Smart' or the Artgineer will be determined by the quality of their thinking, listening skills, relating to others, collaborating with people, locally and globally, and acquiring new knowledge and skills in various new areas. This shift will enable all of us to focus on the hard work of taking our cognitive and emotional skills to a much higher level: to develop our emotional intelligence competencies. This new reality and the new approach to *'being smart'* is where you can see the connection between the three lands.

"And now, before we continue," Rona added, "let me say that in the next land that we'll visit, Sustainability Land, we will build a model to characterize the leaders who will be able to make it through the gushing white waters and succeed in the 21st century. We're scheduled to leave in an hour."

5
Sustainability Land

We almost missed the flight to Sustainability Land. At the last minute, we made it to the gate and boarded the plane. During the flight, I looked out the window and saw steep peaks, wide valleys, mountains and creeks. The beautiful sights from above moved me, and I drifted into thoughts about the experiences we had gone through. For the first time in this journey, I was able to get a fresh look at them. The insights I gathered in each of the places we had visited connected and complemented each other.

Visiting Mindset Land, I learned that the leaders who will succeed in the future will be those who have a growth mindset. It will be those who understand that they don't know it all, who observe and recognize the change, and who adapt themselves to it through constant learning, investment and determination – in all five fields of the '*Whole Advisor*' model. These individuals won't be paralyzed by fear of failure; they will know how to accept mistakes as part of the process.

Visiting Artgineer Land taught me that in addition to

these qualities, leaders in the 21st century will be required to use all parts of their brain. They will have to invest in the development of their weaker parts in order to improve their learning and communication skills and use their personal capabilities to the fullest.

In EQ Land, I discovered the 'emotional intelligence muscle,' which allows for the connection between the various parts of the brain and serves as a bridge between the logical and the emotional. Exercising this muscle creates a better synthesis between intelligence and emotions in the thinking processes, and thus leads to a higher level of self-awareness. When the balance between the logical and the emotional is stable and lasting, it becomes easier to know how to act in any given situation and when to switch gears. In much the same way, this process will also promote social competencies and provide a fuller life experience, as Rona says.

These concepts were no longer gibberish to me, and I could identify their various aspects. The concept of "soft skills" no longer terrified me, and I could see what makes them such critical skills. Yet, the thought that some people were able to meet all of these criteria still sounded quite impossible to me. I wondered whether there were actually such individuals who possessed all of these skills in addition to the high-level professional requirements, which are taken for granted, of course…

I started thinking about the partners and directors in our firm. Pretty quickly I got to John, thanks to whom I was here on this journey. One of the things that characterized him was infinite learning and development. He always said that leaders that didn't learn any new lessons were like basketball players that never practiced and just showed up for the games.

John was always up-to-date with the current professional literature; he had a subscription to management magazines such as the *Harvard Business Review*, and he always insisted on having a professional coach. Clearly, he met the criteria for a learning individual and a '*Whole Advisor,*' something that was very rare amongst partners and directors in our firm. But how were his personal skills manifested?

First, he was highly skilled in everything related to the professional and technical aspects of the profession, as well as to management. He also knew how to get people to follow his lead, and he was always open to listening to others. Second, at any given moment, he could express his personal vision and the firm's vision for the future. He knew how to illustrate a very convincing picture for his team of where we would be in six months or a year. Finally, it seemed like he was definitely using the four thinking styles – the analytic, the organized, the relationship creator and the visionary. With this thought in mind, I fell asleep. By the time I woke up, we were about to land.

Soon after leaving the airport, we arrived at one of the most peculiar places I had ever seen. We came to a large intersection with signs pointing to destinations such as New York, Hong Kong, Georgia, Gujarat and many others. While I was soaking in the cosmopolitan atmosphere, Rona signaled me to walk down a boulevard in the direction marked by the road sign **Tamil Nadu**.

I was familiar with the place, as I had traveled there before my studies, but I couldn't understand what Tamil Nadu in the south of India had to do with our current location...

When we got there, I noticed that the place looked really

authentic. We stopped at a chai shop and I enjoyed the wonderful scents of cardamom, cinnamon and cloves.

"Welcome to Sustainability Land," Rona smiled. "Have you already managed to connect with the creative part of your brain and guess what goes on here?"

"Not really," I replied. "What is this strange place? How come the streets here lead to various locations around the globe, places that are so far away from each other?"

"Well, this is Sustainability land, and it's not a theme park, although it might look like one. This land is devoted to inspiring leaders and pioneers from various fields and from all over the world. Each street or area is dedicated to such a leader and serves as a source of knowledge and inspiration. Through the reconstruction of the places in which these leaders grew up, one can grasp the origins of their beliefs, ideas and actions.

"Business leaders are but a small portion of all the leaders that are represented here. You will also find well-known political leaders and human rights activists such as Martin Luther King, Mahatma Gandhi, the Dalai Lama and even David Ben-Gurion. Rosa Parks, the African-American civil rights activist from Alabama who refused to give up her seat on the bus to a white passenger in 1955, also has a place of honor here.

"In addition to these leaders, who are no longer with us, some of the streets are dedicated to the new generation of political and business leadership. Notice that these places were not created as a place of admiration or worship. They serve as learning and inspiration centers in which one can learn from the actions and accomplishments of great past and contemporary leaders.

"Of all the world's business leaders, I have chosen to focus on a woman who grew up in Chennai, India. Let's hurry and catch a rickshaw to the neighborhood where she grew up."

We went out of the chai shop and into the vivid and bustling Indian street. We caught a rickshaw and passed by busy markets, impressive antiquities, little temples from which the smell of incense emerged, street restaurants with steamy pots and wandering cows. I enjoyed the rhythm of the place and its beauty, mixed with the stench, the noise and the soot. As we entered a suburban neighborhood, the driver announced, "Here we are!"

We paid him and got out of the rickshaw.

"So, this is the childhood neighborhood of the woman I've chosen to focus on. Would you believe that this is the origin of one of the world's most highly esteemed CEOs?" Rona asked.

I looked around and saw white houses with inner courtyards next to a basketball court. It was definitely a middle-class neighborhood.

"This is where Indra Nooyi was born and raised. She now serves on the board of Amazon, but for 12 years, she was the Chairperson and CEO of the food and beverage corporation PepsiCo. She is one of the most influential women in the world. Unfortunately, I don't know her personally, but I'm a huge fan of hers."

"I've never heard that name. How did you find out about her?" I asked.

"That's an excellent question and one that shows what a long way my profession has come... While in the past we would focus mostly on our areas of expertise, today we must pay attention to the business side of things, and not only in our country but all over the world. As a consultant, I try to follow leaders and learn about their actions. That's why I keep myself updated with professional literature, magazines and global conventions.

"I first saw Indra Nooyi at the World Economic Forum,[47] a convention of international political and business leaders such as prime ministers, chancellors and leading CEOs, which is held once a year in Davos, Switzerland."

"Have you ever had the opportunity to participate in one of the Forum's conventions?" I wondered.

"No, participation is very expensive. But YouTube is free, and there you can watch the best lectures from the convention. Nine years ago, I watched a fascinating session about the future of business leadership and the challenges facing organizations in the 21st century. The session was held by former HSBC Chairman Stephen Green, Google CEO Eric Schmidt, China Mobile CEO Wang Jianzhou and PepsiCo CEO Indra Nooyi.

"The four leading CEOs talked about one of the most interesting issues in today's business world. They discussed the fact that economic models have begun to change. During the previous century, a simplistic capitalist concept ruled, according to which the objective of a business was to make as much money as possible, as fast as possible. However, during the first decades of the 21st century, maximizing profit for shareholders is no longer the sole objective. Business success is now measured in terms of business viability, having a stable value and human infrastructure, and serving the society as a whole. These four CEO's talked about the central questions that each organization should ask itself: How do we nurture innovation and arrive first at the best ideas in order to keep on growing, and how do we find the most competent professionals and leaders and retain them?"

"But there are so many powerful and inspirational CEOs," I said. "Is part of the reason you picked Indra Nooyi related to the fact that she's a woman?"

"You're touching on another interesting point, Michael, but that is not the reason I chose her. Indeed, for the first time in organizational history, we are seeing more and more women in key positions in senior management, including CEOs. It's possible that this, too, is a result of global changes. However, I chose Indra Nooyi for the same reasons that *Fortune Magazine* has named her number one on its annual ranking of '*Most Powerful Women in Business*' for five consecutive years, from 2006 to 2010. She's been one of the world's top five leading women for many years. This is a woman who led a thriving global corporation with an annual turnover exceeding $60 billion, up from $35 billion in 2006. Can you imagine that? This amount is much higher than the annual budget of many countries around the world. Still, this isn't why I chose her either; after all, many CEOs have increased the profits of the organizations they manage. As far as I am concerned, there's something special about this woman and her leadership style, thanks to her ability to connect the capitalist-materialistic world with the world of values and higher purpose.

"Indra Nooyi participated in the convention in Davos in the following year as well, in a panel discussion on the future of business organizations, and primarily the way they are perceived by consumers and by people in general and the role they play in the economic crisis."

"In this session, Nooyi turned to Professor Michael Porter of Harvard Business School, a leading authority on competitive strategy, and harshly criticized the training that CEOs and senior executives receive at business schools around the world. According to her, these institutions neglect aspects of social responsibility and long-term thinking. They raise generations of executives who ignore the needs of the environment and the society in which they operate, due to their desire to achieve short-term benefits. She claimed that the mantra of business schools – 'worry about the next quarter' – wasn't valid anymore."

"But the desire of executives to make immediate profits is very natural, isn't it?" I said.

"True. To Nooyi, this desire also comes naturally, or else she would never have succeeded in leading the world's second-largest food and beverage company, while significantly increasing its revenues and net profit. Still, she always says one should aspire to long-term thinking by caring for the environment, the community and the well-being of employees. She claims that doing so actually provides justification for short-term profits."

"And did she implement these principles?"

"Definitely. She did more than just talk; she also practiced what she preached, unlike certain CEOs, whose actions don't comply with their statements. After joining PepsiCo in 1994, she built a whole new strategy for the organization. Under her leadership, PepsiCo started promoting and focusing on healthier products such as natural juices and fruit-based energy snacks. Nooyi also set objectives to improve the health benefits of PepsiCo's products, following criticism leveled at

PepsiCo and similar corporations for their contribution to the obesity epidemic across the globe."

"Unlike the CEOs of other organizations, Nooyi was keen to turn the harsh criticism directed at the corporation she managed into an opportunity for learning and growth. Only a CEO with a growth mindset can do this. She gathered all her senior executives and asked them to become their own critics, as well as listen and try to understand those who criticize them in order to improve themselves. Later, she summoned her harshest critics to meet with her. She told them that even though PepsiCo did not take responsibility for obesity in the United States, they would do their part to encourage a policy that would fight obesity and promote healthy products. She made those commitments despite much criticism from the shareholders, who are less interested in public health and more interested in profit margins. When asked about her policy at a press conference, Nooyi said: 'We invest lots of effort in giving our customers healthy products. Should I regret this? I am proud that we have changed our state of mind.'"

"And how is this related to the success of leaders in the 21st century?"

"Slowly and gradually, we will understand the connection. It isn't trivial," Rona said. "One of the things Nooyi repeats, whenever possible, is that the set of abilities that are important for success in the 21st century will be very different from those required in the past. She came to this conclusion after traveling the world and holding many conversations with various executives at PepsiCo and other leading organizations. She often talks about a 'turning point,' after which the world started changing at a much faster pace. According to her, the turning point occurred in 2007.

"It's important that you understand, Michael – Nooyi is not only an executive CEO and a board member but a true leader. And, as a leader, she doesn't make do with the existing organization and with meeting the necessary schedules. She initiates, leads people through situations of uncertainty and creates changes in a dynamic reality. In many interviews, she is asked what leadership is. She always answers that it is a difficult concept to define and that good leadership is even harder to define. But she has a simple test: if your people are prepared to follow you to the end of the world, then you are probably a great leader."

"How can you become such an inspirational leader if you are not Indra Nooyi or one of the world's leading executives?" I asked. "Is it even possible?"

"Some strategic consulting firms try to provide executives and organizations with tools and insights regarding the road to leadership. In 2009, a groundbreaking research paper was published by Barsh and Cranston,[48] two consultants from McKinsey, entitled 'How Remarkable Women Lead.' Based on interviews with dozens of leading women executives, they constructed a leadership model called Centered Leadership, comprising five dimensions that aid in developing skills and strengths on the road to leadership."

"You said they interviewed women. Are their conclusions also valid for men?"

"Definitely, the centered leadership model has been adopted by many researchers as a model characterizing leadership among both genders. For instance, two senior consultants at McKinsey, Keller and Price, published a fascinating book about the ability of organizations to succeed in the 21st century. They adopted the centered leadership model as a key for leading organizations to success."[49]

"Now you've got my attention," I said, "what is this model?"

"As I said, the centered leadership model consists of **five dimensions**. These dimensions are interrelated in the sense that each one strengthens the others. Together, they serve as tools for leaders whose goal is to build and maintain a sustainable growing business in today's complex and dynamic world. In addition, you will see that these tools are also critical to a leader's own personal sustainability. I suggest that we examine them together from up close and see how the model provides leaders of all ranks with tools that will help them lead in a gushing white waters reality and 'stay on the raft' over time.

"When I was first introduced to the model, I wondered: who of all the leaders today is a living example of this model? I had no doubt that this was Indra Nooyi. In my mind, the path she has chosen brings out the best of each dimension of the model.

"Now let us delve deeper into each dimension and consider its contribution to the success of leaders in the 21st century. We will start with the first characteristic: **Meaning**. Barsh and Cranston argue that a sense of meaning enables leaders to motivate themselves and the rest of the employees at the organization. Leaders with a high sense of meaning feel committed to their work and strive to realize their objectives out of passion and enthusiasm. They are aware of their strengths. They use them and inspire others to do so as well."

"And according to your stories so far," I noted, "Indra Nooyi is undoubtedly a leader driven by a great sense of meaning or purpose."

"True. And if we're talking about Nooyi in the context of the meaning dimension, the first thing I would like to tell you about is the objective-oriented performance methodology she introduced – *Performance with Purpose*. Very early on in her career, she realized that in order to get people to come to work satisfied, or even happy, there has to be an added value beyond the financial profit. This added value is the sense of purpose and direction, or as it is referred to in this model, meaning.

"She started implementing this methodology, based on the two aspects of the meaning dimension. The first aspect is **personal meaning**: It is important for each employee to bring his whole self to work, to be authentic and to find the things that are personally meaningful to him. This will result in both the organization and the employee doing their best for one another. The second aspect is **organizational and social meaning**: It is important that the organization considers aspects of social responsibility and long-term thinking – the understanding that each action comes with a consequence. Every organization acts within human society and should strive to carry out processes that are beneficial to society, rather than abusing it and its resources."

"Do you know if the introduction of this methodology in the organization actually influenced employees?" I asked.

"Certainly, all aspects of the Centered Leadership model have been studied and surveyed by McKinsey.[50,51] Based on 2000 executive's self-assessment of their performance and satisfaction levels, McKinsey discovered that '*finding meaning in one's activities has the strongest impact on general satisfaction*' and that it is '*five times more influential than either of the two closest dimensions*'.

"The bottom line is that each and every one of us requires a sense of meaning both on the personal and on the collective level, in order to arrive happier at the workplace and to give our best. In interviews and lectures, Nooyi has said she is convinced that the sense of meaning motivates not only herself but also her senior executives, their direct reports and, ultimately, the entire organization."

"I wonder what the shareholders think of this process of meaning that she's leading..." I wondered.

"Make no mistake, Michael, the growth of the organization is Indra Nooyi's primary interest, and she knows that this is the center of her business. But she also understands that in order to get there, and stay there for a long time, additional processes should be put in place. According to her, organizations that favor the profit line won't be able to retain it for long, even if they do achieve a positive balance. In other words, a sustainable business cannot rely in the long-term on defining short-term goals stated in terms of growth and profit. As far as she is concerned, business success means a wide and well-based moral and human infrastructure and the establishment of such a sense of purpose and meaning throughout the organization.

"Simon Sinek has a great TED talk entitled 'How great leaders inspire action.' He claims that '*Every single person, every single organization on the planet knows <u>what</u> they do, 100 percent.*' Some employees and leaders know <u>how</u> they do it, whether they call it their unique value proposition or competitive advantage. But only a few people or organizations know <u>why</u>

they do what they do. And by 'why' Sinek does not mean 'to make a profit.' Profit is always a result – a result of a good process. When he asks 'why' he asks about the higher purpose: What is our purpose? What is our deep belief? Why does our firm exist? Why do all the leaders and employees get out of bed in the morning and come to KPMG?

"You should know that most of the researchers studying motivation nowadays agree that it is the end of the era of the 'carrot and stick' approach. Motivation in the 21st century is first and foremost a derivative of a deep sense of meaning."

"It takes a lot of patience and learned optimism in order to invest money in organizational projects that will only bear fruit in the future," I pointed out.

"True, and this leads us to the second characteristic of the centered leadership model, **positive framing**. This dimension enables us to take a constructive and more beneficiary look at reality and to raft forward, even when things are rough.

"This is most certainly a prominent characteristic of Indra Nooyi's leadership, and I think that we need to return to her biography in order to understand it. After earning her master's degree in Chennai, India, she applied for a scholarship at Yale. She arrived in the United States alone, with only $50 in her pocket. And, by the way, when she mentions this in her interviews, she laughs and says that if her parents had believed she would actually get the scholarship, they would most probably never have encouraged her to leave home...

"Nooyi worked as a receptionist to support herself during her studies and saved up cent by cent. This is a woman who immigrated to a foreign country on her own, and who lived far from her family and friends in difficult economic conditions.

There is no doubt in my mind that her ability to positively frame difficult situations assisted her on her road to success."

"I wonder if she used this capability, as CEO of a large international corporation," I said.

"Sure," Rona answered. "After all, the business world is extremely volatile, especially in a time of turbulent economy. As CEO, she had to cope with failures, declining sales, layoffs and harsh criticism from shareholders. It is not that she didn't realize the difficulties and hardships. But being the CEO, she knew that she shouldn't display any signs of anxiety or distress.

"On the whole, being the leader that she is, although she has a realistic view of the situation, she also knows that giving up is unacceptable. She understands that the management has to identify growth opportunities and convey optimistic information about these opportunities throughout the organization. She refers to this attitude of seeing the glass half full as 'realistic optimism.'

"As you know, many people lost their jobs during the recent economic crisis. PepsiCo employees were also worried and wondered about their own fate. Nooyi realized that the mood she instilled in the organization would have an immediate effect on the executives and employees, especially on their productivity, and thus made sure to positively frame the situation. She conveyed a strong message throughout the company that things were all right. She justified her optimism by pointing out the fact that they were a consumer staple company, which would not be highly affected by the crisis since people still buy food, even during a downturn."

"Do you think that this optimism, this positive framing, is a trait she always had?" I asked.

"Interviews with Nooyi make it quite evident that the feeling that there would be no limit to her accomplishments in life is, after all, something that she received through her education at home. Her mother instilled in her the belief that she could achieve whatever she wanted and encouraged her to dream big. Most definitely, growing up with parents like this has a tremendous influence on you."

"This reminds me of our insights from EQ Land, about Jacob and his learned optimism," I noted.

"Good point. Many people believe that learned optimism is a kind of manipulation by individuals who are not bright and talented enough. I can tell you without a doubt – pessimistic individuals suffer from laziness of thought. It is so easy to see what is wrong, what is not working, what could go wrong. As an advisor, I say this to all the leaders I work with, as I try to teach them to focus on what is currently working and what may succeed in the future. This is a critical ability that is required for the continuous and sustainable success of any organization or individual.

"But make no mistake. In a changing reality such as ours, in the eye of the storm, one of the most important abilities of a leader is to be able to read the changing reality and face it as it truly is. On the other hand, it is equally important for a leader to instill learned optimism in his staff. The leader must show faith in his staff and their ability to succeed, despite the temporary difficulties they may face. Learned optimism makes a substantial contribution in any change process, Michael, and especially in significant ones. After all, if you don't believe that success lies ahead, why even try?"

"I would like to remark, Rona, that the two dimensions

of the model you mentioned so far, sense of meaning and positive framing, sound to me like characteristics you either have or you don't."

"This is arguable," Rona replied, "and the world's best researchers, including Martin Seligman, would disagree with you. But let's get to the third dimension, which most certainly can be developed and perfected. This characteristic is called **connecting**, and it means the active construction of an array of connections with other individuals, inside and outside the organization. It's well known that people with a larger and more complex social network enjoy better conditions at work. They make more money, get promoted faster and derive greater satisfaction from their work."

"This is also related to what we've learned in EQ Land, and particularly to interpersonal abilities," I said. "And at this point in our journey, I have no doubt that it is a critical ability in the world of advisory."

"You are right. You should also know that Nooyi argues that emotional intelligence is one of the most important competencies for leaders. And this comes from a woman who regularly appears on the lists of most influential women in the world and tops the list of most influential CEOs.

"Now, let's examine her performance in the context of connecting with other individuals. What is noticeable about her is that she has a vast network of connections with other CEOs, senior consultants, heads of state and regulators. However, when asked about the main skills that are important for a CEO, she always answers that it is the ability to connect with talented and young employees. She talks a lot about Generation Y, about their constant need to be on the move and switch jobs for promotion. According to her, executives who are capable of associating themselves with their young employees by adding an emotional aspect to the connection will be able to retain their excellent employees."

"Of course," I answered.

"Michael, I think that Indra Nooyi definitely seems like a leader who knows the extent to which people are a central component in the success of the organization. And she doesn't use this knowledge in a cynical way, as many executives do."

"How do you reach this conclusion?"

"Here is an example: after being appointed CEO of PepsiCo, she went to her hometown in India for a party her mother was throwing in her honor. She was excited to meet her friends and family, in her new position. The interesting thing was that the guests who attended the party came to her mother first, rather than to her. They congratulated her mother and showered her with compliments and admiration for having raised such a wonderful daughter, who brings honor to Chennai and to all of India. That day she realized that parents, who work so hard in raising their children, making sacrifices, caring for their well-being and their success, are usually not acknowledged when their children finally do succeed.

"She decided to turn this understanding into action. Upon returning to the United States, she wrote a personal letter to the parents of her executives, in her own handwriting, describing their achievements, activities and contribution to the success of the organization. She also wrote about the things that PepsiCo does to help make the world a better place. She says with a half-smile that some of the parents even started corresponding with her. You can surely imagine what it felt like for these parents to receive such a letter, and consequently, how their children, the senior executives, felt."

"Wow, I'm trying to imagine my mother receiving a flattering letter about me from our senior partner. She'd be very pleased, although it feels kind of awkward. Nonetheless, Nooyi sure sounds like an extraordinary leader in terms of how much she cares for others."

"I agree. And it is this kind of concern that drives employees and creates motivation. It is what increases their sense of capability and achievement, and gives them a feeling that they are worthy and indispensable, thus enhancing their commitment to the organization and its objectives. It may surprise you that motivation is not related to the size of your bonus, but rather to your sense of meaning and your relationship with your manager. Nooyi's care for her employees is related to the fourth dimension of the model – **engaging**.

"The concept of engagement incorporates commitment and involvement. It is our ability to listen to our inner voice, to trust ourselves, to initiate and act without the need for approval, and to get others to act under conditions of uncertainty and risk. And what are those conditions of uncertainty and risk, Michael? Well, most of the conditions today are just that."

"And how is this dimension manifested in Indra Nooyi?"

"Nooyi has always said that she is stern and demands a lot from herself, and this filters into her environment and eventually raises the bar for all those around her. According to her, only individuals who take complete ownership of their development and organizational activity can lead an organization to success over a long period of time. She believes that as CEO, you lack the privilege of resting on your laurels. CEOs must constantly learn and develop since reality is constantly changing. Nooyi believes that we should always aspire to be the best, and we should be aware of the fact that this requires a never-ending process of learning and evolving, as part of a professional's daily life. Anyone who fails to do so will probably be incapable of maintaining his competitiveness over time.

"She sometimes jokes about the fact that CEOs don't have a written guide to teach them how to manage an organization with a turnover of $10 billion, $20 billion or $50 billion. They are forced to write the book as they work. As CEO, she is expected to make difficult decisions under conditions of uncertainty, and this requires great physical and mental efforts. She doesn't sleep more than four and a half hours a night, and most of her time and energy is spent on leading organizational strategies.

"Indra Nooyi was definitely an involved CEO. As CEO of PepsiCo, she was highly in tune with the organization she led. In her own words, 'I am a walking ad for PepsiCo.' She never hesitated to go down to the manufacturing floor for a close examination of her business decisions. A great example of this approach is her trip to China before PepsiCo entered the Chinese market. She went into houses, stores and restaurants in order to become intimately familiar with Chinese consumption habits."

"And what do you mean by 'the ability to listen to your inner voice'?" I asked.

"She's not afraid to think differently and says that each and every one of us has a compass that should direct us and our actions. She is well aware of the strong influence she has on her organizational environment, as well as on her social-global environment. She uses any platform she can to present her beliefs, and argues that one of the roles of global organizations is to cooperate with governments and make the world a better place."

"Rona, you said earlier that she insisted on promoting healthier products, in spite of the reservations of the members of her board. I assume that this is what you mean when you speak of listening to your inner voice."

"Exactly, Michael. I'll give you another example of her commitment to her principles, and of the fact that she doesn't bow down to external pressures. During her first year as CEO of PepsiCo, the members of the board expressed their dissatisfaction with the expenses related to implementing an objective-oriented performance methodology. She didn't panic but stayed loyal to herself and to her own path. Her answer was that this was the only way she knew how to manage a corporation on the scale of PepsiCo."

"I can understand the members of the board," I noted. "Like any group, they also fear changes, especially when these changes also cost so much..."

"But remember, Michael, that striving for change doesn't mean that you're unsuccessful. It means that you're always searching for new ways to learn, to continuously improve and make yourself fit for the changes imposed by reality."

"Honestly, Rona," I confessed, "from the picture you're painting here, I would never want to trade places with her.

You said yourself that she gets only four and a half hours of sleep a night. It sure sounds like she has no life outside of work. What about leisure, family outings, friends, hobbies?"

"Right you are. I also ask myself how she and other executives of her stature manage to survive for so many years in such a demanding position that doesn't allow you any time for yourself."

"So, how do you explain it?"

"I believe it has to do with the sense of meaning we discussed earlier, as well as with **managing energy**, the fifth and last dimension of the model. Understanding how to manage and channel our energy is a key factor directing our actions and the way we practice our profession, and helping us gain emotional well-being. As I said before, it isn't necessarily related to money, but to resources such as leisure, friends and more.

"With such a demanding job, it's hard to say that any CEO of a large company, such as Indra Nooyi, has an abundance of emotional well-being. However, any knowledgeable person understands that it's impossible to work for a long time at that pace without constantly maintaining and generating energy. I believe Nooyi has a few ways of doing this. First, like any executive, she understands that when we choose a demanding career, it comes at a price. But even in this demanding world, she is capable of taking care of herself."

"So how does Indra Nooyi take care of herself?" I asked.

"First of all, just from looking at her, it appears that she really enjoys what she's doing. When we're dealing with things we love and are good at, there is a sense of flow."

The word 'flow' reminded me of the spiritual experience

that people talk about when they return from India, but as Rona continued, I realized this wasn't what she meant.

"The concept of 'flow' was defined by psychologist Mihaly Csikszentmihalyi,"[52] Rona continued. "Flow is '*a state of concentration or complete absorption with the activity at hand and the situation*' while feeling that nothing else matters. There is great pleasure when we delve into this kind of activity that takes us to the point where time just flies by and we forget everything else, undisturbed. In such a situation, when we're completely submerged in the moment, our performance is enhanced. In addition, after we complete the activity, we don't feel exhausted but rather charged with energy."

"I understand exactly what you're talking about," I pointed out. "I also love my job. But what else keeps Indra Nooyi going for so many years as CEO?"

"When asked what the secret of her success is, she always answers that it is her family, friends and faith. Indra Nooyi is married and is raising two daughters. She has a circle of friends, and she also has faith. These are the sources of her energy."

"Well, Indra Nooyi definitely sounds like a real wonder woman," I smiled.

"I know it sounds too good to be true, but believe me, she is indeed exceptional. She has a combination of hard and soft skills, high cognitive and strategic thinking abilities, along with high emotional intelligence. I have no doubt that there are many in the business world and in business schools that find her unusual, as do I. She inspires whoever listens to her and to her principles, which she actually lives by.

"When she was interviewed for an article about the

requirements from executives in the 21st century, she said that as far as she was concerned, it was a privilege to head the organization she was leading. She said that every day, on her way home, she asks herself what it was that earned her the privilege of being CEO, and what new things she has learned. I believe that each and every one of us should ask himself these questions, regardless of the position or path we choose to define our success. Do you know a lot of executives who ask themselves these questions at the end of the day?"

"I recognize that she is indeed a remarkable woman," I agreed. "I must say that the combination of abilities, as you describe them, definitely sounds critical for CEOs or senior partners. Yet, I also feel that it is less critical for directors and even for most partners. We don't need to manage everything, and we most certainly don't have this kind of influence or impact, which is typical of the work of a CEO such as Indra Nooyi. For this reason, I'm not entirely convinced that the model of centered leadership is relevant for me."

Rona looked at me for a long time. "We are nearing the end of our journey, Michael. At this point, you should be able to answer these questions on your own, rather than wait to be given answers. Take a few minutes and try and think of the five dimensions of the model in the context of your own personal experience. This exercise could assist you when you get back to work."

I thought about it for a few minutes and then I shared my thoughts with Rona. "The first dimension I can think of is **connecting** with other individuals. At this point, I realize that this is one of the most important abilities for success, not only for partners or senior partners, but also for directors like me. Every leader must connect with others: team members, superiors, consultants, colleagues and interfaces at other organizations. I remember that John once asked me to work on a joint project with an executive from a large global corporation, and it was a complete failure. In the aftermath, I realize that this failure derived from my inability to connect with him on a personal level. I had no clue, at the time, that what really mattered were our relationships and the mutual commitment that comes with them.

"I definitely think it's important that I carefully learn how to build relationships that are based on trust. I must surely learn how to become someone who helps others and puts them and their needs in the center, rather than my own goals or needs; someone who actively listens to them and truly wants to understand their perspective and needs. I also need to learn how to make my interactions more meaningful in order to build this trust. I fully realize that the world is going in the direction of large work teams from various disciplines, and there's no doubt that I have to develop more empathy, listening skills and mental flexibility to be able to succeed in these teams.

"That's a beautiful and excellent analysis, Michael. What about the other dimensions?"

"Regarding **positive framing**, as we have said all along the way, leaders today have to deal with an extremely challenging reality, charged with uncertainty. In my daily work, I too have often encountered situations in which it appeared that we had gone back to square one. It sometimes even reached a point that I had absolutely no idea what could be done.

"On the other hand, I remember seeing Ron, one of my

colleagues from the international tax department, assembling his team and instilling them with motivation, letting them know that if they took the necessary steps they would be able to succeed in spite of all the difficulties. At the time, I thought he was deluding his staff with unrealistic promises.

"Today, I understand that it is optimism that enables us to continue to row in the white waters despite the difficulties. That means that part of my job as a leader is not only to describe reality as it really is, but also to highlight the positive points, everything that works well, in order to lead to a better situation. This also makes it clear to me what the role of a leader is in times of crisis when you have to get out of the gushing white waters and back on the raft. I have no doubt that Ron used positive framing in order to help his team deal with their difficulties.

"Slowly but surely, I'm starting to see the connection between this dimension and a sense of meaning. I now fully agree that I have to strengthen my self-conviction and my sense of meaning in my profession. I also understand that the more I am connected to my inner compass, the more I will be able to effectively attain positive framing.

"As for **engagement**, I must say that up to now, this dimension only guided me with regard to the professional aspect. Now, I realize that I must expand it to other aspects, interfaces and processes. This understanding has been accompanying me from the first land we visited, ever since learning about the 'Whole Advisor' model. When I return to work, I plan on seriously developing all the aspects of the model. And I don't mean only the parts relating to management skills. I plan to invest more time in my ability to connect with other individuals.

"I also realize that I need to have a vision for myself. I plan on taking full responsibility for my development and learning process – to build an organized personal development plan and set goals, actions and timeframes for every component and dimension we discussed. I also realize now that it is important to make my voice heard and say what I think, even if my view is different than others, in a constructive and collaborative manner.

"Deep down inside, I know that I'm capable of this. I feel resolute and committed to the process, because this is what sets apart meaningful leaders from those who will soon become irrelevant."

"What about the dimension of **meaning**?" Rona asked.

"I must honestly say that I have never thought about the sense of meaning as an element related to my success at work. Last year, Martha led the project of 'My KPMG Story' in which every leader and employee shared what working at KPMG means for them. I really felt that it was a waste of precious time. Now I understand that success, in any area, will belong to those who actually find a deep sense of purpose in their everyday work. Those who strive to accomplish their goals, those who don't give up in the face of difficulties, and above all those who do business with a purpose. Over time, in such a challenging and obstacle-ridden reality like the one we live in, you won't keep going if you don't have a sense of meaning to guide and strengthen you. So, with these understandings in mind, I've started to formulate my own sense of meaning, dividing it into organizational meaning and personal meaning, inspired by Indra Nooyi.

"At the organizational level, it is clear to me now that our purpose is to Inspire Confidence and Empower Change. Through our audit work we inspire the confidence of our clients and their investors, strengthening the capital markets and economies in which they operate. Through our tax work we help maintain balance between individuals, institutions and governments, essential for a fair and thriving society and through our advisory work we help our clients transform, bringing our skills and experience to empower them to make positive changes in their business and in the world at large.[53] Now I can see very clearly that our purpose at KPMG is a timeless description of who we are, why we exist, our history, culture, values and the role we play in the world. With regard to our organizational culture at the office in our everyday life, this exactly reflects who we are.

"At the personal level, as a director, considering my team members, it is clear to me now that my role as a leader is to pass on to my team members everything I've learned on this journey. Among other things, I should help them discover their personal purpose – their own story. Also, I should help them develop a growth mindset attitude in the five fields of the 'Whole Advisor' model in order to become Artgineers, and to cultivate their emotional intelligence.

"Up to now, the only sense of meaning I was able to appreciate was related to ambition – to succeed by being promoted to the next position and making more money. I now realize that if I truly find my sense of meaning in self-development and leadership, aspects that are on more of an inner level, it will ultimately lead me to whatever I wish to achieve.

"And as for the final dimension, **managing energy**, I relate it to what we talked about in EQ land, about how feelings are contagious. I can remember those partners who came to work filled with vitality and positive energy and made us all feel the same way. Meanwhile, others arrived at work drained, and this made us feel the way they did. If I want an upbeat, energetic team, I have to work on my energy levels. The first thing that I want to do when we get back is to swim. I haven't been able to find time for this ever since my last promotion. But before that, I used to wake up with energy and enthusiasm and go swimming for an hour. I remember that it certainly made me feel much more energetic and vibrant. I also want to spend more time with my wife, Mia. Today I realize that if I do this, it will certainly improve my ability to go to work the next day with higher levels of energy.

"I now understand the close connection between my energy levels and the energy levels of my team. I realize that one of my most meaningful tasks as a future leader will be to create this sense of energy with my team. I am certain that the best way to do this is to work with each team member on their personal sense of meaning. I will try to thoroughly understand what's important to each and every one of them, and I'll try to motivate them through it. Most importantly, I will try to inspire a sense of enthusiasm in the team and create an organizational culture that is based on enthusiasm. And, of course, I will also pay attention to the other important aspects of this dimension, such as sleep, nutrition and sports.

"Personally, if I can connect to the sense of meaning we

spoke of earlier, and if I remember how much I really love my job and how good I feel about it, I will be able to feel many moments of flow, just like Csikszentmihalyi described it. This sense of flow is also a source of energy.

"I also know that when I feel energetic, it is easier for me to dare and face new and challenging issues, as well as my own fears. As a leader in the 21st century, I will most certainly get bogged down without it."

6
I-21

"And now, Michael," Rona said, "I have a surprise for you. We have spent so much time talking about the infinite journey leaders take toward success in the 21st century. Now, before going on to the fifth and final land in your private journey, you have a once in a lifetime opportunity to see yourself in five years' time."

"You mean I should write a summary about where I would like to be in five years?" I hesitantly asked.

"No, no, I mean you can actually **see** yourself in five years' time. We are going to visit the hi-tech labs of FutureSym, the inventors of a unique simulator capable of showing you yourself in the future, based on your current characteristics; a kind of a virtual realization of a future reality. When we get there, a technician will give you a helmet and connect you to electrodes that will read your data. The simulator will then evaluate your readiness for management in the 21st century."

After a rather long trip, we reached the labs. We went into

a dark and cozy room where we met Patrick, our technician, who greeted us with a large smile. "You're lucky, Michael," He said. "You have a rare opportunity to experience your life five years from today."

I asked about the connection between his work and the concept of "vision" and whether the opportunity to clearly visualize the future would make it more attainable. Patrick thought for a moment, and said, "This process is indeed based on studies on the power of vision and visualization. It means that if we can imagine our future reality in a detailed manner, our chances of getting there are multiplied. The helmet you are about to put on will make you see your thoughts five years from now as if they were a movie. You'll actually be able to see what you're thinking!"

Suddenly, I was afraid. What if I didn't like what I saw?

Patrick read my mind and said, "Look, the process works in a way that lets you start whenever it's convenient for you. Normally, your thoughts will wander at first, and it will take time to calm them down. When you feel you can focus them and tune-in to the future, you can press the red button and start seeing clear images."

He connected me to the electrodes. My heart was pounding. It took about 20 minutes before I felt I could press the red button and start watching myself five years from today. I took a deep breath, focused and pressed the button.

The first images that appeared were very similar to my life before I set out on this journey. I remembered what Rona told me about changing mental maps, took another deep breath and focused on our journey together. Our experiences from the four lands we had just visited went through my mind. I recalled the people, the sights and the smells, and only then did I dare take another look at the simulator.

The image before me became clearer. A complete day of my life, five years from now, passed before my eyes. At first, I saw myself sitting, as a partner, at the head of a long table with 20 other partners, directors and managers, leading a discussion about one of our biggest strategic clients. I noticed the positive atmosphere in the room, the open conversation. It was apparent that everyone in the room enjoyed their work. I saw how each and every one of the participants felt comfortable while openly expressing their thoughts, and how each and every one of them assumed personal responsibility for the project. At the end of the meeting, one of the directors came up to me and asked me if we could move his mentoring session to an earlier time, as he had some important things he wanted to discuss with me.

Towards lunch, I saw myself sitting with the Tax and Advisory teams discussing our part in fulfilling the firm's strategy. I could once again feel a positive atmosphere. The tax partner asked to update the staff on changes that were going to be put in place in the coming month. It seemed like everyone understood the importance of this and cooperated.

Next, I saw myself meeting one of our strategic clients in the senior management meeting room. The client, a CEO of a large company, talked about the pressing issues currently on his mind. From time to time, he asked for my opinion regarding this or that process that was being implemented in his organization. He looked at me with an honest and welcoming look, from which I understood that I had been able to build a significant relationship, based on trust and proximity with this man, and become his trusted advisor.

I was happy to find out that I was the first person he turned to in times of need. Throughout our meeting, I used more than my professional expertise, and it was noticeable that he recognized and appreciated the fact that I used high organizational and interpersonal skills.

In the next image, I saw myself leading a major change process in the firm. There I was, standing in front of all the directors and partners in my department, applying the four thinking styles, trying to answer the questions of each of the participants in the language that was most effective for them. I was talking about the vision behind the change, about the reasons for changing our objectives, about schedules, about figures, about the emotional consequences the change would entail for each and every member of the staff and for our clients. I saw myself positively framing the situation at hand, or in other words, doing my best to lead the raft through the white waters.

Most of all, I felt that each one of the participants felt and understood that we were all part of a team that works together, in cooperation and harmony, in order to live and fulfill our purpose and achieve our vision. It looked like we managed to create a winning culture and were truly living the KPMG Story. I felt extremely satisfied.

Finally, I saw myself leaving work at the end of the day with a feeling of fulfillment and satisfaction, and I was looking forward to the rest of my day with Mia and our two children. Just before taking off my helmet, I asked myself the question that Indra Nooyi asked herself – have I earned the right to be the head of this department today?

I had no idea how long the helmet had been on my head – it

could just as easily have been an hour, five hours or a whole day. I left the room and saw Rona looking intrigued. "How was it, Michael? Were you able to see yourself in five years' time?"

This was the first time throughout the journey that words failed me. "It wasn't easy, but yes, I did. It was a fascinating experience."

"And how are you feeling?" she asked with interest.

"I have mixed feelings," I answered. "On the one hand, I really enjoyed watching the leader I am going to become, but on the other hand, I'm not sure that I have what it takes to actually become that leader."

Rona smiled, "I'm happy that you got to see yourself in five years' time and that you liked what you saw. This simulation definitely points to the fact that you are on the right track. It confirms what I thought from the start – that you have what it takes to become a true leader in the 21st century."

I was surprised. "How come you never told me that before? Had I known that you had faith in me, I would have felt more secure, and this entire journey would have looked different..."

"The answer to your question is related to the fifth and final land, **I-21**."

"**I-21**?"

"Yes, meaning '*me in the 21st century*.' From this name and its meaning you can understand that **I-21** looks different to each and every one of us. All the insights gathered in the previous four lands lead to our own **I-21** land and are expressed through our personal, professional and organizational activities."

"Wait, so actually... You don't need to travel a long way to investigate it?"

"Not only do you not have to travel a long way, but in order to get a proper look at it, you simply have to go back home, to your daily life. In two hours we will board a plane back home. Upon returning to your daily routine, you will start a journey to the most fascinating land that man can ever reach. Everyone can go to countless beautiful and interesting places, but no journey is as exciting as the journey of self-discovery, self-development and self-creation."

"In that case, I understand that the journey through **I-21** is not limited in time..."

"True. The journey through your personal land never ends, and it is obvious that as you begin it, you will understand that everything we went through was just a setup for the real deal. You are returning home with insights that give you a good starting point for proper orientation in this land. Just remember that we are not talking about a toolbox, as there is no ready-made toolbox for the 21st century. The key is flexible and adaptable thinking, enabling dynamic balance. In the past, people went through various processes to 'discover themselves' in order to find a direction in life. In the 21st century, this is insufficient. In order to succeed, people will have to 'reinvent themselves' and even 're-engineer themselves' once every few years.

"As Professor Yuval Noah Harari mentioned in one of his interviews talking about his new book, *'21 Lessons for the 21st Century',* the only way to make sure that we stay relevant and continue to participate in the game is to reinvent ourselves, regardless of our age and position. No one these days has the luxury of holding on to some fixed identity, job or world-view. By trying to do so, you risk being left behind as the world flies by."

"I'm starting to envy explorers like Columbus and Marco Polo... They set out toward the unknown as well. But at least their goal was evident to them – new lands, natural resources, commerce routes, new cultures..."

"That's exactly the point. In the 21st century, the unexplored areas won't be physical. Therefore, in order to succeed, people will have to reinvent themselves and lead a similar process in the organization they work in."

"And how am I supposed to do this?"

"This is no doubt a challenging process which requires plenty of awareness, investment and perseverance, but I believe that you're already equipped with the necessary tools in order to go through it."

"I already have awareness, that's for sure. But what do investment and perseverance entail?"

"The way to recreate ourselves begins with a simple **mirroring process**. For the process to be effective, it is important to make it a routine, part of your everyday. Throughout the process, you must clear half an hour of your time at the end of each day, and recreate the day you went through and the meaningful events you took part in. Choose a place where you feel calm and ask yourself a few questions based on the lands we have visited:

- With regard to the five fields of the 'Whole Advisor' model: In which events throughout the day did I display a growth mindset and in which events did I stick to a fixed mindset?
- In what situations throughout the day did the "artist" part of me, as an advisor and a leader, rather than the "engineer" part, come into play? Did I use all four parts of the brain – the analytic, the organized, the relationship

builder and the integrative? Which of them were more dominant, and did they serve me well?

- Which EQ subscales did I use today? Which mental muscles served me? And at the same time, which muscles are relaxed and need strengthening?
- Did I emphasize the five dimensions of the centered leadership model and did I develop the skills and the strengths required of a leader in the 21st century?

This daily mirroring process is the investment required of you in order to stay on the right track. Perseverance means that you have to keep on doing this as a habit for life, just like your decision to swim every day."

These many questions echoed in me. I took a deep breath. "I understand that I am supposed to reinvent myself. But who will be there to help me if I get stuck? Who will assist me in practicing the growth mindset, sharpening the four parts of the brain, exercising the relaxed EQ muscles, and acting according to the five dimensions of centered leadership?"

Rona, who apparently understood the source of my concern, answered in a relaxed voice, "First of all, I think you are going to need far less help than you think. And second, you have Martha, John and me. We'll continue to assist you on your journey towards becoming a leader in the 21st century."

"Even the daily mirroring process alone seems demanding, Rona. The questions you posed sound heavy, and it's not clear to me where I can fit them into my tight schedule..."

"I agree with you, the mirroring process is demanding at first. But in a few weeks you will enter a coaching routine, and by then it will take you less time and will become a sort of daily inventory. I guarantee you that it's worth the effort because this is the key that will provide you with an edge over others.

"In my eyes, self-development is a mandatory tool enabling you to see yourself clearly and examine your progress, to identify patterns managing your life, to know your skills, your fears and your barriers. Addressing these issues will enable you to develop to a higher level of self-awareness and to find the necessary patience in your stressful routine. The mirroring process will assist you in understanding when to lead and when to stay behind, when to take responsibility and when to learn to trust others. It will also show you how to become an authentic person. Authenticity, Michael, is overwhelming. It makes you the person everyone wants to do things with, no matter what. Naturally, this will also project on your personal life, your children and your *joie de vivre* in general."

"Rona, I'm still trying to figure out why you didn't tell me, at the beginning of the journey, that you believed in my ability to succeed and to lead. Did you want me to find this out for myself?"

"Exactly. I didn't tell you what I thought, as I strongly believe that one of the most important talents for a leader is self-leadership and lifelong learning. The need for reinforcement is natural, of course, since we all like to hear compliments and kind words from those around us. But these words cannot be the source of our motivation. As a leader, you must develop your own sense of significance, security and clarity, which will enable you to act without depending on constant approval from everyone. And that is what you did on this journey. You've undergone a meaningful personal process without expecting support or reinforcements. Your achievements are all yours, the process is real and noticeable, and now you will get positive feedback, but it won't be your source of energy, your fuel. Whether you get reinforcement or not will not be the only factor that will either motivate or paralyze you, because you have yourself and your own insights."

"Yes, I'm beginning to figure that out…"

"And now, Michael, it's time to go back. I have no doubt that the mental and emotional process you went through on this journey will assist you in creating your own I-21 land. Let's grab a taxi to the airport. We wouldn't want to miss our flight. There are plenty of people waiting for you at home."

7
Back to Work

Rona definitely convinced me of the importance of this **mirroring process**. On the plane back home, I took my calendar in order to clear out half an hour from my schedule every evening, assigning it to a daily follow-up session. As Rona recommended that I sit in a quiet place, I immediately thought of Café Ana, our neighborhood café, with its pleasant simplicity. For years, ever since I was a student, this cafe has been my favorite spot. As a person who loves cafés, I sat in many other places, but Café Ana is my homeport. I go there whenever I'm searching for a quiet and private place in the heart of the city. I sit at a table facing the window or on the comfortable couch, and after the first sip of cappuccino, I can feel a sort of flow of productivity and creativity. Certainly, this was the ideal place to do my daily mirroring.

I returned to work two days after Rona and I excitedly said our goodbyes, promising each other we would meet again. The return from my fascinating journey wasn't trivial. I admit that I couldn't sleep all night long due to my excitement towards the first day back at my "normal" life. Lying awake in bed, I revisited the people I met, the scenery I saw and the experiences I had during my journey. I was curious to see how my staff and colleagues would welcome me back. I missed everyone, and I was filled with joy and curiosity in view of the expected reunion. I was eager to implement all that I had learned on the journey; but I also promised myself I would not be like those who have "seen the light" and cannot help themselves from expressing their opinion on every matter.

In the parking lot, in front of the building, I felt I had returned to a familiar place. I walked inside and went up to my department. Everything looked the same, but the feeling was different. I took a fresh look at the colorful paintings in the halls, and I noticed the great effort that was put into designing our offices. The colors reminded me of the first half of Mindset Land. Many questions raced through my mind during those moments. First and foremost, I wondered whether I really was successful in my journey. I wondered whether it would be possible for me to change my old habits, to think and act differently over time and to implement all that I had learned. Would I become a worthy leader?

On the flight home, Rona and I had a long conversation. I remember that she emphasized, over and over again, that this journey was infinite. The work that we do with ourselves should be something that doesn't stop at any point. She also said that if we did a good job, we would be able to really feel it, as something inside would feel different. I had no doubt that part of me had already changed, but I still needed someone or something to indicate that I was on the right track.

The meeting with my team was especially exciting. They

were happy to meet me, and it was obvious that they had missed me. From the moment John had told me that I would be in charge of them and their career development, I felt this was an important role. But it was only on my journey that I realized how important it was to lead and train them in a profound and comprehensive way, and I couldn't wait to start helping them develop the five fields of the 'Whole Advisor' model. After having coffee together and telling old and new jokes, I scheduled lunch with each of them in private. Throughout these conversations, I felt that my speech had changed and that I was using the terms I had acquired during the journey. I asked open questions so I could learn about their situation and their ability to 'make it' in the changing world of the 21st century. In this way, I could learn what needed improvement and how I could support them. I noticed that, unlike before, a significant part of the conversation revolved around personal issues, some related to work and some not.

Slowly, after the initial suspicions dissolved, they started cooperating and responding to me, opening up and sharing things with me. It seemed that they were eager to have a meaningful conversation with one of the leaders in the firm. This type of conversation had never existed in the past, as I was the one in charge of their personal and professional development. I felt satisfied with the new ability that I acquired, to see things I hadn't seen before.

I have always cared deeply for my team, and this had not changed. But, in addition, I felt a much greater sense of responsibility for them and their career development. As a result of my journey, I now understood that I had a personal responsibility, as their leader, to see that they underwent the coming changes in an effective manner and that they would not be left behind.

During these personal conversations, I realized for the first time that Harry, seemingly the most brilliant manager, had a fixed mindset. I saw how it "bogged him down" in various processes at the firm – with the KAM methodology, with the DPP and with the clients. For the first time, I realized that the very fact that our most talented accountant had a fixed mindset was an obstacle to innovation, hindering our efforts to improve our services, and standing in the way of him realizing his full potential. After being exposed to his rigidity of thought, I suddenly understood why everyone opposed his ideas even though he was more talented than all of us put together, professionally speaking. Since I was familiar with his many professional virtues, as well as his strong ambition to be promoted, I couldn't help but feel a sense of missed opportunity. I realized that nothing could be done at this moment to promote him, even though he was highly professional. Thinking about ways to help him, I realized that nothing could help Harry more than a journey to Mindset Land, so he could realize how much he would benefit from leaving his comfort zone and developing a growth mindset.

Then, I noticed how Sophia, a highly motivated manager who was adored by her team, arrived every morning with a smile on her face. I also noticed how beautifully she worked with others, how remarkably open she was to feedback and how she often asked for it from her surroundings. I saw how she set challenging objectives and left her comfort zone without any effort, how she invested hours in setting goals and achieving them. I admit that I didn't appreciate her properly before my journey; neither did I give her much attention, as she appeared less sharp and brilliant than the others. But now, I rediscovered her, understanding that she has what it takes to succeed – a sense of meaning, positive framing, readiness for effort and investment, high-level interpersonal skills and the ability to dare, to take chances and to grow. These are all of tremendous importance when one is trying to succeed in the ever-changing reality of the 21st century.

This led me to think of the story about the "ten-thousand-hour rule" that Rona told me, and about the musicians at the Berlin Music Academy. I decided that I had to tell it to my staff. I had a feeling that Sophia could be an ideal partner in the process that I was about to lead among my staff. I was certain that she was the most suitable candidate for promotion. She had proven herself to be persistent in making efforts to get better and more professional.

In my conversation with Ethan, I noticed that his interpretation of the project and its status showed that he only used the left part of his brain. I saw how he relied solely on facts and figures, always checking the applicability of things and searching for certified proof, in a sort of close-up examination. His total disregard for the ideas and feelings of his staff, who brought forth new ideas that were outside the box, and his inability to coherently communicate his thoughts and connect them to the bigger picture were also evident. I also noticed that he lacked the ability to answer any question about his staff at the personal level, neither to address the issues that bothered each of them. Ethan undoubtedly required plenty of help to successfully progress and change his attitude. Clearly, visiting Artgineer Land would be very relevant for him.

I was excited about my new ability to examine situations from the points of view that I had acquired on the different lands we visited.

An hour hadn't gone by, and I received a long e-mail from one of our strategic clients, with a serious complaint about Joel, another member of my staff. The client wrote that he was rather satisfied with the technical aspects of the project, but was disappointed and even hurt by Joel's manner of speech and from the way he treated him, and asked that he be replaced. This was not the first time that a client had complained about a member of my staff, but this time the source of the problem was clear to me, as well as the type of process I had to go through with Joel. If in the past we treated complaints as a nuisance that got in our way, I now understood that these types of complaints and dealing with them in a proper and educational manner would lead our department to live by our mission statement every minute and every hour. I finally realized that it was the client who paid my salary at the end of the month, and for this reason I should find a way to provide him with the best value proposition I could. I knew that we had to do our best to be the clear choice for our clients.

I invited Joel to meet for coffee the next week to share some of the insights I had acquired in EQ Land with him. I felt that I couldn't just call him to order, as I had in the past, but had to guide him and teach him how to conduct himself. I could help him acquire the necessary skills for dealing with our clients and being the clear choice for our clients.

As time went by, I realized that I was able to see each and every one of my staff members, and especially myself, in a new light – a light originating from the lands I had become acquainted with during my journey. The staff meetings we had held in the past, which focused on professional issues and technical details, now seemed highly incomplete and one-dimensional; they lacked essential information necessary for the success of all of us. I decided that I must start thinking about ways of making the staff meetings more significant so that they could successfully lead us, as a team, through the white waters that lay ahead. I started planning the steps necessary to help my team members adopt a growth mindset, use skills from the four parts of the brain and incorporate their soft skills at work.

In view of the events and the conversations I had with my team since my return, I realized that there was still much work ahead. I felt I had been given a gift and must "Pay It Forward." So, I opened the first folder of 2020 on my computer and named it "*The Five Lands Journey with My Staff.*" Then I opened a new document and started typing in all the insights that I would like my staff to internalize.

Before embarking on my journey, I asked Rona how I would know that I had passed the journey successfully. Now, her answer echoed – "You will know it once you can't keep all the insights you have acquired to yourself; when you have a tremendous urge to share them with the rest of the world; when you come back to work and strive for all your nearest and dearest to internalize these insights; when you don't understand how it is possible to think or act otherwise. Then you'll know you have successfully taken the journey and have become a leader fit for the 21st century."

For the first time, I had a fresh new look at my job and realized the scale of its complexity. It was obvious to me that I would continue to need orientation and support, and the first person I could think of was Martha. I also realized that I had to use all my insights in a deliberate way and start the change in my staff, using all the emotional intelligence skills I could. I needed to create the conditions that would make them want to set out on such a journey with me, without deterrence or resistance. In order to do so, I felt like I needed as much help as I could get.

I remembered the anger and frustration that engulfed me after my last meeting with John, when he said that I needed help and direction if I wanted to be successful. At the time, I tried to postpone getting help, as it seemed like admitting failure. Now, I yearned to receive more advice in order to manage myself more effectively and wisely. I felt fortunate to get this opportunity for a change, and I also experienced an entirely new sensation. I was thankful to John – thankful that he literally forced me to face this fascinating challenge. As I walked toward John's office, I was full of excitement.

"Welcome," John said as I entered his office. He greeted me with a hug and a smile. "I had a long conversation with Rona and Martha, and we concluded that you were one of the best travelers in recent years. You should also know that not all leaders survive this journey. I'm sure that your management experience will now be entirely different, as will our next feedback session.

"You know, five years ago, I went on that same journey.

I went through similar experiences, and I also felt the need to share them when I returned. I would be delighted for us to schedule regular meetings to share our insights and to exchange our impressions."

But it wasn't only my encounters with the team and with John that changed. As I returned home to Mia, I knew that the change I had gone through in my journey wasn't limited to the workplace, but continued into my personal life. Those same insights were just as relevant to my relationships with Mia and with my family, friends, acquaintances and service providers. The ability to accept the diversity of people, to learn from each and every one of them, to understand that my feelings affect my whole environment, to stay optimistic in times of pressure and assertive enough to get things done without offending others – these were all as important outside of work.

In the past, I felt illiterate, with no direction in this new world of skills that I didn't understand or appreciate. Now, I felt that I had the tools to succeed in it. As I started to think passionately about the challenges I was facing, I realized how everything was connected. Surely I could make a significant contribution to my team, be successful and help lead the firm forward. Filled with feelings of significance and satisfaction, I promised myself that I would keep developing and maintaining the insights I had acquired in order to keep waking up every morning like I did today – enthusiastic and energized. The true journey has only just begun, but I knew I had the right toolbox to succeed, I thought on my way to Café Ana...

PART B:
Q&A
Theoretical Background for Success in the 21ˢᵗ Century

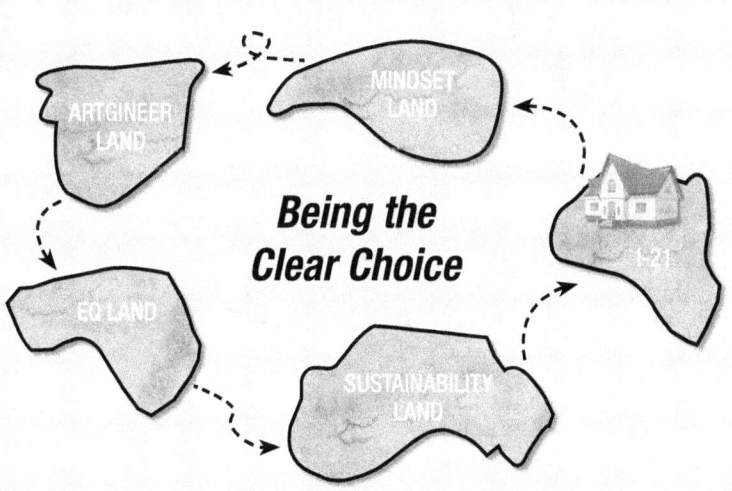

Mindset Land

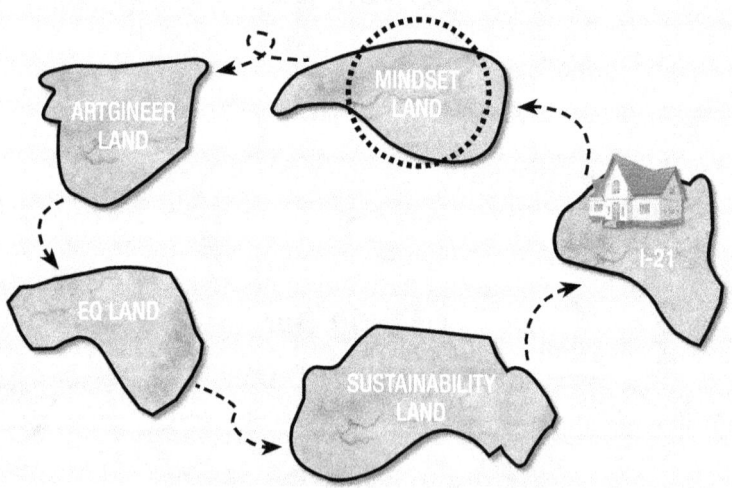

Questions for Thought and Reflection

Think about and explain to what extent you agree (or disagree) with the following statements:

1. Our abilities are innate, hereditary talents and there is nothing we can do to change them.

2. Failure is not the end of the world; however, remaining stagnant, unwilling to make any effort, does indeed constitute failure.

3. It is possible to attain great achievements through passion, enthusiasm and hard work.

4. It is highly important to try and conceal (or disguise) our flaws so that the people around us think we are perfect.

5. People are constantly changing and evolving. If you don't – you will become irrelevant.

6. One should never try something new unless he's at least 90% sure to succeed.

7. It is important to do everything we can to ensure others perceive us as smart, talented and successful.

Mindsets

"Just as organizations are going to be forced to learn, change, and constantly reinvent themselves in the twenty-first century, so will increasing numbers of individuals. Lifelong learning and the leadership skills that can be developed through it were relevant to only a small percentage of the population until recently. That percentage will undoubtedly grow over the next few decades."

John Kotter

1. What is the meaning of the term "mindset"?

The term "mindset" originates from decision theory and general systems theory. According to Professor Carol Dweck from Stanford University, a mindset is the set of assumptions, views and attitudes held by an individual (or group of people) that determines the manner in which they approach situations, interpret them and respond to them.[54]

A mindset is essentially our mental roadmap, telling us what to do and how to act in any given situation. Often manifesting itself as an inclination or a habit, a mindset is also described as a "paradigm" or mental inertia. Our mindset is the result of many factors such as the education we received from our parents, schools and environment (society), and the values they imparted to us.

2. Who coined the terms fixed and growth mindset and on what basis?

The term was coined by Professor Carol Dweck based on more than 20 years of research.[55] A substantial part of her work was done in schools, where she observed and compared successful and failing students.

Dweck discovered that the most prominent characteristic of students who succeeded in school was their perception regarding "wisdom" and "intelligence": they believed that both could be developed. Most of them were confident that their skills and achievements consistently improved as they put in more effort – trying harder, asking questions and practicing. However, the failing students believed that wisdom and intelligence were innate skills which they could not influence. They thought that no matter how hard they studied or practiced – they would always get the same results.

In other words, the successful students believed that they could influence the situations they faced. They believed that effective handling of challenging circumstances would lead them to success. The failing students, on the other hand, felt helpless and unable to influence their fate and believed that they were destined to fail.

Dweck argues that our mindset deeply influences our achievements in all stages of our professional and personal lives. She calls these two types of mindsets, which characterize failing and successful individuals respectively, *Fixed Mindset* and *Growth Mindset*.

3. How are the two different mindsets related to the world of management?

While some executives believe that leadership is an innate skill that cannot be improved, others argue that leadership is an acquired skill that can be developed by investing efforts and getting the proper orientation.

Apparently, this seems to be part of the same old debate about whether we are a product of nature or nurture. Today, most researchers agree that we are a product of both. However, the interesting thing about what Carol Dweck discovered is that any individual's answer to this question has a direct impact on their achievements in life! This renders the "correct" answer to the old debate entirely irrelevant.

In other words, the mindset of executives, whether fixed or growth, deeply influences their achievements in both their professional and personal lives. The attitudes of executives differentiate between those who become who they wish to be – those who are capable of achieving their objectives – and those who do not.

4. What are the attitudes of individuals with a fixed mindset toward the basic concepts of success, talent and effort?

- **Skills and talent:** Individuals with a fixed mindset believe that their skills and behavior are hereditary and permanent and cannot be changed or developed.
- **Success:** Success serves as proof that they are smart and talented. It enables them to get as much external positive reinforcement as possible about what and who they are.

- **Failure:** Situations like rejection are experienced as failures. Failure proves that they are incompetent.
- **Investing effort:** People who are competent do not have to put in any effort. Such effort would expose their flaws and show that they actually lack the skills required to accomplish their tasks successfully.

The result:

People with a fixed mindset spend their lives – at work, at school and in their relationships – searching for validation of their intelligence, personality and character. They assess themselves in every situation: will I succeed or will I fail? Will I be perceived as wise or stupid? Will I feel like a winner or a loser?

In situations of failure, these people "fall apart" as if the situation is beyond repair. They deduce that they are not worthy because "they didn't make it" and that it is futile to keep trying. They fear challenges and do not believe in the value of their efforts. They are afraid to leave their comfort zone and are reluctant to undergo or accept any significant change. When confronted with such a situation, they will do anything to hide their disadvantages and will invest vast amounts of energy to convince everyone around them that they are extremely talented.

5. What are the attitudes of individuals with a growth mindset toward the basic concepts of success, talent and effort?

- **Skills and talent:** Individuals with a growth mindset believe that they will be able to nurture their essential qualities and succeed – through desire, dedication and effort.

- **Success:** Success is measured in the ability to broaden their horizons in order to learn and develop.
- **Failure:** Remaining stagnant, being unwilling to put in any effort to fulfill one's own potential is considered as failure.
- **Effort:** Development through self-challenging, learning and training throughout one's life is the key to success.

The result:

Individuals with a growth mindset believe that each and every one of us can change and evolve. They see life as a journey and believe that what they do not know today, they will learn tomorrow, or the next day, or the day after...

They believe that the real potential of an individual is unknown and that it is impossible to predict where one might end up. This belief creates a passion for learning and development, for seeking challenges and overcoming disadvantages rather than concealing them.

To them, an expert is an individual who made every possible mistake in a very narrow field. As a result, they are always seeking ways to step out of their comfort zone. They neither desire nor need to prove that they are talented, and they invest their time and effort in constant improvement.

6. What are the characteristics of executives with a fixed mindset?

- They believe neither in their own ability to change nor in the ability of others to do so. Therefore, they reject any change or demand to improve on their weaknesses.

- They fear challenges and do not believe in the value of their efforts.
- They fear failure and fear being perceived as incompetent, and so they "play it safe" and only do what they're sure they will succeed in.
- They are worried about how they are perceived by others, and consequently, they constantly seek significant positive reinforcement.
- They will do all they can in order to be perceived as smart, talented and successful.
- They believe that every organization has superior and inferior individuals, and they will do everything to prove their superiority.
- They let their ego manage them in their relationships with others.

All this is liable to:
- Have an adverse effect on their effectiveness and performance at work.
- Increase their general lack of trust and resistance to change.
- Limit their creativity, innovation and problem-solving abilities.
- Have a negative impact on their health, happiness and emotional well-being.
- Make them less and less relevant to the organization.

7. What are the characteristics of executives with a growth mindset?

- They believe everybody is capable of improving and developing. Consequently, they invest considerable effort in their self-development, as well as in that of their subordinates.
- They see problems and challenges as opportunities and consistently invest considerable effort to overcome them.
- They learn from their mistakes and failures.
- They are open to criticism and encourage feedback.
- They often seek new and challenging experiences.
- They are attentive to everyone around them (executives, subordinates and consultants) as they believe that there is something to be learned from everyone.
- They communicate with those around them with respect and treat them as equals.
- In stressful situations, they employ a sense of humor and optimism.
- They succeed in spite of the difficulties.

Therefore, individuals with a growth mindset:

Know that not everyone can be an Einstein, but are also aware of the fact that their potential is unknown in advance. They believe that training, enthusiasm and a passion for what they do can lead them to extraordinary achievements. They are aware of the fact that avoidance of training, development and growth might hinder the realization of their potential as leaders, senior executives, scientists or champions.

8. Is it possible to develop a growth mindset at any age?

Certainly! People can develop a growth mindset at any age. The first step is recognizing the two different mindsets and the heavy price people with fixed mindsets pay for their beliefs. After all, we are talking about beliefs, and one can most certainly change them. In his workshop for executives, Peter Heslin asks participants to answer certain questions and perform certain tasks, such as:

- Think of at least three reasons why it is important to realize that people can actually develop their abilities. Prepare a five-minute lecture for your team.

- Think of a former area of weakness of yours – an area where your performance was weak in the past but in which you perform better today. Explain how you brought about this change.

- Write an e-mail to a hypothetical protégé or apprentice who is in a difficult spot in his career, sharing examples of how you dealt with challenges in your career and proposing ways to develop his abilities.

- Recall when you last saw an individual learning to do something they never thought they would be able to do. Think about what happened, how it happened and what it means.

9. How are mindsets related to the success of executives in the 21st century?

As discussed, the 21st century is characterized, more than ever before, by constant and rapid changes. The most important ability one can have in a changing reality is the ability to learn and adopt new habits and new patterns. In the 21st century, executives will be required to leave their comfort zone and expand it on a regular basis.

Executives with fixed mindsets will soon find out that their value proposition for the organization is decreasing, since they object to any process involving significant change or learning, particularly with regard to their own abilities. These executives do not perceive themselves as "inventors" and thus will not be able to help their organization reinvent itself and win in a competitive world. They perceive the road towards the unknown, with all the possible failures that lie ahead, as almost traumatic.

On the other hand, executives with growth mindsets will invest considerable effort in studying and developing new areas. They will dare to leave their comfort zone and creatively assist the organization to reinvent itself whenever necessary. They will do so themselves and lead their staff to adopt a similar approach and join them along this path. These executives will lead successful changes.

10. How are mindsets related to the successful execution of changes in organizations?

When John Kotter wrote his first book, *Leading Change*,[56] only 30% of organizations were able to execute effective changes. Today, after almost two decades, hundreds of books and thousands of articles later, these statistics are still valid. How come? The answer probably lies in the ability to implement change.

In his book from 2008, *A Sense of Urgency*,[57] Kotter argues that the biggest mistake in the traditional model of leadership lies in its basic premise that leadership is an innate skill, "a divine gift of birth," rather than an acquired one. He notes that this perception is not in line with his own observations from 30 years of research and experience with organizations and individuals. According to Kotter, this early model does not take into account "the power and the potential of lifelong learning."

When Kotter talks about the 21st century, he adds: "In the twenty-first century, I think we will see more of these remarkable leaders who develop their skills through lifelong learning, because that pattern of growth is increasingly being rewarded by a rapidly changing environment."

Today we know for sure that if we focus only on the behavioral aspect of change, we will probably waste our time and energy because **the behavior of executives and employees is a result of their mindsets.** However, we also know that changing the behavior of individuals is the most significant challenge facing business organizations trying to compete in a world dominated by changes and turbulence. Therefore, in spite of the difficulty of changing one's mindset, it is the only way to create real change.

11. How can executives help their employees develop a growth mindset?

Executives have great influence in shaping the mindsets of their employees. In order to establish and reinforce a growth-promoting state of mind in their teams, executives must create the atmosphere that supports it in a number of ways:

- Setting a personal example and serving as a model for the behavior of an executive with a growth mindset.
- Transforming "lack of success" and "failures" into

"learning processes" and "opportunities" for reflection and change.

- Remembering that talent is not the most important characteristic of employees. Rather, what matters most is their attitude and the effort they put into their tasks. Thus, they should be positively reinforced for their efforts, learning and determination.

- Encouraging their staff members and creating a secure environment so they may be more able to handle difficulties.

- Encouraging their staff members to take calculated risks in order to be creative, think 'outside the box' and create new and effective processes – to develop the next trend, the "next big thing" in their field.

- Responding to the failures of staff members as opportunities for learning and development – conveying the message that failure is not the end of the world and that we all make mistakes.

- Establishing personal development plans, together with staff members, that precisely define the current status, the objectives to be accomplished throughout the quarter, and the measures required in order to do so.

- Developing a training program based on the organizational strategy and the employees' objectives, and focusing on the skills that are important for success.

- Providing quarterly feedback to every staff member in which attitude, effort, determination, expressions of creativity, and the willingness to take chances (at the risk of making mistakes) are emphasized.

12. Is there such a thing as an organizational growth mindset?

Definitely! Mindsets exist at the organizational level just as they do on the personal level. An organizational fixed mindset is one of the reasons that many executive development programs fail to achieve their goals even though hundreds of thousands of dollars are invested in them.

In organizations where a fixed mindset is prevalent, those who return from training are often discouraged from implementing what they've learned. They hear remarks from their managers such as *"What we do here is real life; forget all those classroom theories you have just learned and come back to reality."* Such responses by senior management negatively affect the behavior of their subordinates more than anything else. As a result, they relapse into their old habits, or convey a message to their own team members that is counterproductive to the necessary changes and to the organization's best interests.

On the other hand, in organizations where a growth mindset prevails, managers and employees know that development and learning are important. They realize the need to proactively adjust to a changing reality. Consequently, such organizations invest in the design of change processes and appropriate training programs.

These programs must be aligned with the organizational strategy and its objective and must provide tools, skills and proficiencies to help people go through the change. Further, any such program must start at the top to be successful since senior management must energize the process and support any new practices. Such support should be reflected in their actions, as well as in their interactions with their subordinate executives and employees, upon their return from their training. A growth mindset organization continuously devotes resources to secure its future and its objectives.

Recently, the Harvard Business Review has published an article called 'How Companies Can Profit from a "Growth Mindset"' which extends Carol Dweck's work on mindset from individuals to organizations.[58]

First, Dweck and her colleagues studied the existence of an organizational mindset and found that companies do possess "a real consensus" which forms a collective mindset of employees. Some companies are characterized by a belief that their employees have a certain fixed amount of innate talent and cultivate a culture of "star" performers. Other companies hold an opposite view and regard talent as a dynamic property, the result of learning, practice and experience.

Following this result, the characteristics of each type of organizational mindset were studied. Among the surveyed issues were the workers' satisfaction, levels of collaboration, innovation, ethical behavior and more.

The fixed mindset companies were found to foster a culture in which only the "star" workers get recognition, credit and reward. The other employees felt less valued, less "backed up" and were, therefore, less committed. The price that such organizations pay was striking, starting from keeping secrets to cutting corners and cheating.

On the other hand, in the growth mindset companies, the employees were found to be more committed to the organization and willing to pursue innovative projects. They were more collaborative and spent less time on politics.

13. How is an organizational mindset created?

Usually, an organizational mindset is created and transmitted without words or intention. A good example is a famous experiment described by Gary Hamel in his book *Competing for the Future*.[59] The experiment demonstrates how experiences from the past and present become a future behavior or tradition.

In the experiment, four monkeys were put in a cage. Bananas were hung from the top of the cage, which could be reached by climbing a staircase. However, each time the monkeys tried to climb the staircase towards the bananas, a water hose sprayed a strong stream of water at them. A few days later, the monkeys gave up on their attempts. At this point, the researchers disconnected the hose and replaced one monkey with a new one. When the 'new' monkey noticed the bananas, he tried to climb the stairs, but the other monkeys pulled him down to protect him from the water splash. After the monkeys repeatedly prevented him from climbing up to the bananas, the 'new' monkey stopped trying, though he didn't understand the reason.

Over the next few weeks, the researchers gradually replaced all the monkeys with 'new' ones until there were no more monkeys who had actually witnessed the water splash. The researchers continued to replace old monkeys with new ones. Even though no one knew the reason (the water hose, which was removed), whenever a new monkey tried to climb and reach the bananas, the other monkeys pulled him down. They had all learned the rule – one mustn't attempt to reach the bananas...

A similar phenomenon takes place in organizations: employees avoid acting in a way that might improve performance merely because they are used to the way things are done, and any other way is considered wrong!

14. How can an organizational mindset be changed?

It is important to understand that it is impossible to change a mindset relying solely on facts that are different from those that shaped the mindset. When facing facts that contradict our beliefs and mindset, we label them as wrong, irrational, unnecessary or even silly.

In his book *Changing Minds*,[60] Gardner points out six R's – six leverage points for change that have to work together for the mindset to change:

- **Reason:** When we try to influence others, it is highly important to provide them with a reason for the change.
- **Research:** One should present evidence based on relevant studies and supported by numbers, and, if possible - on statistical analysis as well.
- **Resonance:** Creating an emotional bond: people need to feel that the change is right for them in order to foster positive feelings towards it. Therefore, they must be connected through emotions: by presenting the desired idea, point of view or vision through a story.
- **Re-description:** A multi-dimensional presentation: a different opinion (or point of view) is more convincing if it is presented in several different ways: through a story, graphs and open questions. The various ways support each other.

- **Rewards:** Even after the need for a change of mindset has been established and accepted, and even when people are emotionally connected to the leader of the change and to the new concepts – one must wisely use resources and rewards (material and other) to support the new way.
- **Real world events:** This leverage is outside of our domain of influence. It includes worldwide events that might affect all of us, such as recession, natural disasters, war or peace and prosperity.

Objections

It is important to remember that since mindsets are formed at a young age, it is hard to change them, and naturally there will be objections. Only when the six leverages work together in harmony will the pattern start to change.

Questions for Mirroring and Development

1. When recently did you dare to do something in a new and innovative way?
2. When was the last time that you really left your comfort zone? In what circumstances?
3. Which ability that is important for your success have you developed over the past few years? Who helped you?
4. What was the "most significant failure" or "lack of success" you experienced throughout your career? What did you learn from it? How did you cope with it?

5. What really excites you? How is this excitement expressed?

6. What are your prominent weaknesses at work? Who other than yourself recognizes them? And how do you cope with them?

7. People are constantly changing and developing; when you look around you, who do you recognize as the individual who underwent the most significant change over the past two years?

8. In what areas do you put in most of your effort at work?

9. What did you think and how did you react when you encountered the following situations:
   • Another executive in your group is being praised for an accomplishment.
   • As part of a feedback process, you were told that you need to significantly improve particular skills.
   • A direct subordinate of yours wanted to share his thoughts about the last project.
   • You tried to cope with a task (or project) and had no idea where to begin.

10. If you had to explain, **to your son or daughter**, the importance of having a growth mindset in order to succeed in school or at work – what would you say?

Artgineer Land

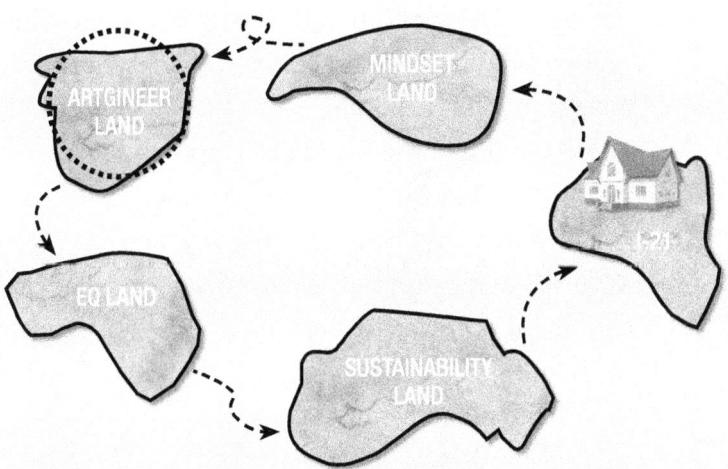

Questions for Thought and Reflection

Think about and explain to what extent you agree (or disagree) with the following statements:

1. There is a strong correlation between the occupation we chose and our brain tendency.

2. Our brain preference may be an asset or a drawback, depending on the situation.

3. Every professional must strive to become an "Artgineer."

4. Each of us can strengthen the weaker parts of our brain through exercise and practice.

5. As leaders, our success (both professional and personal) relies only on the left, cognitive side of the brain, while our success as leaders requires the use of all four parts of the brain.

6. Understanding others and their brain preferences assists communication and cooperation.

7. The abilities to effectively work as a team as well as retain employees and clients are dependent on emotional skills that are related to the right side of the brain.

8. In order to develop our weaker aspects, we require a growth mindset.

Artgineer

"The brain is the most complex thing we have yet discovered in our universe."

- James Watson

"21st century organizations need not just half a brain – but a whole, full, complete brain, where both halves work in unison and harmony."

- Umair Haque

1. What is the origin of the "Whole Brain" concept?

When discussing **the Whole Brain** concept, we are essentially talking about the division of the brain into several physical (as well as conceptual) segments. However, there is more to the concept than brain structure. Above all, it is about how one's ability to effectively use all parts of the brain will lead to a fuller realization of one's potential and to much greater success.

Basically, the Whole Brain concept relies on and develops from studies of brain function lateralization (the physical division of the brain into two hemispheres, each characterized by different functions), aiming to describe and understand different thinking styles which are complementary to each other.

Therefore, in order to introduce the Whole Brain model, we first need to understand the two hemispheres concept and related model. Daniel Pink, in his book *A Whole New Mind*, phrased it as follows:

- **The left, rational hemisphere** is related to analytical and logical abilities, language and arithmetic, factual information and time perception.
- **The right, metaphorical hemisphere** is related to abstractions and associations, identification of nuances, fitting data into the bigger picture, interpretation of sensual data and handling spatial functions.

According to this model, people have different ways of absorbing and processing data, which influences their decision-making and behavior. Our thinking style (and consequently, our mindset) reflects the dominance that a certain hemisphere has in our thinking processes. Also, as stated earlier, our mindset influences our abilities, our relationship with ourselves and our environment, and our decision-making process.

It should be noted that the aforementioned theories of the brain reflect a metaphor for how individuals think and learn. The use of this metaphor later resulted in criticism from brain researchers, who claimed it was overly simplistic. In practice, although overly simplified by "pop" psychology, this metaphorical construct has proven useful in many organizational contexts such as education, business and government. This model is useful in describing different tendencies which are related to different functions of different parts of the brain, and, therefore, to different thinking styles.

2. Who created the Whole Brain Model and what was the model based on?

Ned Herrmann, a trained physicist and musician, took the theory of the lateralization of brain function and developed it into the Whole Brain Model.[61] He developed his model while serving as head of Management Development at General Electric, where he had to cope with issues that concern all executives: how to increase employee productivity, motivation and creativity.

First, Herrmann relied on extensive studies regarding the different specializations of functions related to the left and right hemispheres of the brain that result from the longitudinal fissure (which separates as well as connects them to each other). Then, he expanded the model by adding an additional dimension that results from the well-documented specializations of the cerebral cortex (which is responsible for cognitive functions) and the limbic system (which supports functions such as memories and emotions).

Thus, he created a four-quadrant brain model, with each quadrant resulting in a different thinking style and consequently in different reasoning skills and interaction styles. The proportional use of these four thinking styles shapes our mindset and our approach to solving various problems.

It should be mentioned that the above-mentioned theories of the brain reflect a metaphor for how individuals think and learn. Use of that metaphor brought later criticism by brain researchers for being overly simplistic.[62] However, this metaphorical construct has proven useful in many organizational contexts, such as education, business and government.

3. What are the components of the model?

The integration of a second dimension in the two-hemisphere model results in a four-quadrant model and, as a result, in four patterns or styles of thinking and behavior.

Each of us has one or two dominant thinking styles that shape our mindset and our approach to problem solving. They also influence our relationships and our decision-making processes. In fact, studies show that the population is pretty much equally divided between these thinking styles.

4. What are the characteristics of each of the four thinking styles?

Before characterizing the thinking styles, it is important to realize a few basic facts:

- The distinction between the various thinking styles becomes evident early on in our lives.
- The different thinking styles are neither good nor bad. Rather, they may be either an asset or a drawback, depending on the situation and on the way we use them.
- Thinking styles are not rigid: most people are capable of using a mixture of styles and approaches and are not limited to a single and narrow thinking style.

- People are capable of learning and expanding their range of behaviors and thinking styles. In certain situations, they can deviate from their usual style and act differently.
- Understanding the thinking styles of others assists individuals in communication and cooperation.

The characteristics of each of the different thinking styles, detailed in the tables in Chapter 3 of this book (Artgineer Land), come to play in everyday situations at work – in interactions with clients, in communication with staff, colleagues and managers, in professional activities as well as in leading strategic changes.

Below is an example of the differences between leaders who present a new issue in a meeting with many participants – the differences in how they manage the meeting, as well as in the points they choose to emphasize and highlight, according to each of the four thinking styles that characterizes them:

A. Logical & Analytical Self

Before the meeting:

- Goes over all the graphs, numbers, data and facts to check that there are no mistakes.
- Prepares measurable and rational arguments in response to questions that might arise.
- Prepares a presentation packed with graphs and numbers.

During the meeting:

- Presents all the data and makes sure that everyone understands it and its significance, but then goes directly to the main issue.
- Talks about ways to implement each part of the process.
- Leads the participants in a logical way to the required conclusions.
- Uses technical aids and gadgets throughout his presentation.
- Finishes by summarizing the technical objectives that the group must reach later on.

B. Safekeeping & Organized Self

Before the meeting:

- Goes over schedules: what was planned and what really occurred.
- Reserves a meeting room of the appropriate size and place.
- Sees to the availability of technical instruments.
- E-mails everyone about the time and place of the meeting and asks them to be on time.

During the meeting:

- Goes straight to the issue at hand and to his presentation.
- Presents what has been accomplished as planned and what hasn't, with great accuracy and reliability.
- Finishes by setting a new schedule for the remainder of the work and planning the different parts and areas of responsibility.

C. Feeling & Relational Self

Before the meeting:

• Googles meeting participants to learn about them.

• Takes care of refreshments and beverages.

During the meeting:

• Uses sophisticated small talk throughout the meeting.

• Conveys warmth and concern and makes all the participants feel good throughout the meeting.

• Empathically listens to each of the participants and asks questions in order to better understand the existing reality.

• Compliments the ideas of others and provides them with positive reinforcement.

• Schedules the next meeting for lunchtime.

D. Explorer & Experimental Self

Before the meeting:

• Thinks about the significant accomplishments he wishes to make; prepares creative and colorful posters to assist him in conveying the main issues and convincing the participants.

• Prepares himself using a few creative, out-of-the-box solutions to problems raised at previous meetings, thus providing participants with the opportunity to make a choice.

• Arrives at the meeting in a good mood and full of energy.

During the meeting:

• Opens the meeting with a holistic top-to-bottom description of the current status.

• Asks questions in order to understand where the participants would like to see themselves by the end of the project.

• Uses intuition in order to promote important concepts.

Always finishes the meeting on an optimistic note.

5. Is it possible to map one's cognitive style or preference based on this model?

Definitely. Based on this scientific concept, Herrmann built an applied model for the evaluation of thinking styles (the HBDI).[63] The characterization of an individual's dominant thinking style is based on a test designed to evaluate their preference of (or tendency toward) one or more of the thinking styles associated with the four quadrants. While this evaluation tool examines mental tendencies rather than competencies or skills, it is known that there is a strong correlation between one's tendencies and competencies. This correlation exists because the dominance of a particular part of the brain influences our level of interest, the development of our preferences and interests, our motivation and our skills.

6. How does knowing our preferences help us?

Each and every one of us possesses a unique composition of thinking styles. Understanding our personal cognitive style or preference is an asset, as it enables us to be aware of our strengths and weaknesses. This knowledge allows us to focus on the development of dormant skills in order to make them available to us in times of need. Awareness of the various thinking styles enables us to maximize our personal skills, through better communication with our environment and by acquiring a toolset of effective learning and problem-solving techniques.

7. Is there any correlation between our occupation and our thinking style?

The profession we choose is greatly influenced by our thinking style. At the same time, the profession we choose deeply affects our thinking style. Unsurprisingly, most of us choose a profession that rewards our preferences and enables us to expand our skills.

Using the HBDI survey, which was tested on about 200,000 professionals, Hermann was able to characterize 200 different groups of professionals by isolating and measuring the strength of their preference for each of the four thinking styles. The profiles built for each of the professions indicate a **strong correlation between thinking style and work preference.**

Engineers and economists are mostly dominant A types, while librarians and production managers are mostly B types; the dominant C type characterizes social workers, elementary school teachers, customer-service employees and volunteers; artists are mostly D types. The dominance of C-D (right-brain) tendencies characterizes counselors, psychologists and clerics. Meanwhile, CEOs of large companies are mostly characterized by a tendency to evenly use three or even all four thinking styles.

8. How is the model related to the world of management?

Whether he defines himself as a leader, an executive or simply as a manager, if we look at the reality that today's managers face in any executive position, we will discover that they are required to use all the thinking styles in a balanced manner.

Today's executive is required to work with diverse interfaces in his own organization and in other organizations with which he collaborates. In many cases, he has to connect with people from various countries and cultures, through various interfaces. In addition, he must work with different types of customers and retain strategic clients. Often, he is required to implement a strategy and organizational vision and to lead changes.

To fully understand the reality in which they operate and to effectively execute all their tasks, leaders must undoubtedly use both the cognitive and emotional parts of the brain. One cannot keep his good employees or his strategic clients unless he has an emotional connection with them. Graphs and schedules do not retain any of them; however, relationships based on trust and significant added value, definitely do.

9. Can the "weaker" parts of the brain be developed?

The "weaker" parts can most certainly be developed through awareness and training, although this is not an easy process and one must usually invest much time and energy to do so.

For instance, a leader with an AB thinking style who is about to lead a change should not speak of facts alone (such as numbers, schedules, outputs and measures of success rates), but must also address employees with a CD thinking style, providing answers to questions that trouble them: To what extent will the change influence their future? How does the change fit into the bigger picture? Why is there a need for change? Can they influence the process? What will be the implications for their clients? Who will be available to listen to their concerns? Will they be able to personally relate to the change, and if so, how?

10. Can we talk about the four parts of the brain at the organizational and departmental levels?

We can indeed. Organizations and the organizational culture that exists within them can be characterized according to the properties attributed to the four parts of the brain. In the 21st century, organizations, like people, will need to use all the parts of the brains of their executives and employees in order to reinvent themselves.

Today, it is reasonable to assume that most organizations are dominated by thinking styles characteristics of the AB quadrants, meaning that they exhibit high levels of skills and capabilities related to the left part of the brain. While focusing on the bottom line, organizations of this kind operate using methodological processes that are based on figures and preplanned schedules, timetables, facts and projections.

Accordingly, many organizations lack a holistic approach based on leaders capable of creating an original and challenging vision, merging various ideas and taking risks. Moreover, many organizations lack leaders with good interpersonal communication skills, capable of functioning well in a team, mentoring and supporting others, communicating through global interfaces within and outside the organization. In the 21st century, just like people, organizations will undoubtedly have to use all parts of their "collective brain" (the combination of their managers, employees and organizational culture) in order to reinvent themselves.

On the other hand, in organizations where the organizational culture is based on the four parts of the brain, one will also see an emphasis on a sense of purpose, effective communication and relationships between staff members, as well as on the self-fulfillment and well-being of staff members. These organizations normally have a formal or informal vision that includes both the hard and soft aspects of the profession.

11. How is the Whole Brain Model related to success in the 21st century?

In his book *A Whole New Mind*, Daniel Pink characterizes today's Western society as a society on the verge of change, whose essence is a transition from the knowledge era to the conceptual era, and even to the creative era. In this new age, success and even survival undoubtedly require the adoption of mindsets and approaches that are different from those that were prevalent in the past.

The experts of knowledge will no longer be able to 'deliver the goods' on their own. In order to prosper, a wider approach will be needed, integrating all thinking styles, even those that were underestimated in the past such as intuition and creative thinking. These qualities are expected to open up new ways of competition in every field.

Skills and technical knowledge will remain central, but in many cases they will be performed by computers (automated systems) and through offshoring (outsourcing work to lower paid employees overseas). Meanwhile, executives at the head of the organizational hierarchy will have to handle wider issues that require creativity, adaptation and innovation.

Intuitive thinking and interpersonal skills such as empathy will be important traits in the future economy, as they will distinguish between successful and mediocre organizations. That is why individuals who are capable of merging various disciplines (such as observing and understanding others, creating purpose and significance, telling a story or even transforming activities into games with goals) are the ones who will become essential. Individuals who will be wise enough to adopt the leading values of the conceptual age and to train employees with a wide creative vision will find new opportunities and new marketing channels in the 21st century, and will determine the state of mind of modern life.

The great complexity that has come to characterize the organizational world, has created a built-in need for executive positions that are designed for leadership, and particularly for leading change.

This trend forces 21st-century leaders to use all parts of their brain, as their work has become much more complex. This change, in fact, marks the end of the management era and the beginning of the leadership era.

In the management era, high-level ability (and even dominance) in the use of both parts of the left-brain was a necessary prerequisite. In the leadership era, at the beginning of the 21st century, an additional prerequisite for success is remarkable right-brain competence, i.e. a whole-brain outstanding performance.

A leader must work with people – connect with them emotionally, create a sense of trust and empathy and make them willingly walk the extra mile for him and for the organization. Many studies point to the fact that people are not actually committed to organizations, but rather to their managers. In his book *Drive*,[64] Daniel Pink discusses how leaders can imbue their employees with motivation in three ways: expertise, autonomy and meaning. Without a doubt, only executives who succeed in using all four parts of the brain will be able to do so.

In his book *The Future of Management*,[65] Garry Hamel notes that the abilities that contribute the most to the success of business organizations are passion (35%), creativity (25%) and initiative (20%). They exceed intelligence (15%) and diligence (5%). Obedience, which was also tested, makes no contribution to organizational success. That's right, 0%! It is therefore clear that organizations need leaders who can excite their employees and develop an organizational culture that encourages creativity and enables (and empowers) employees to be flexible, autonomous and show initiative. These leaders must use all four parts of their brain.

Another aspect that characterizes management is related to the fact that managers work with clients on a daily basis. In such a world where you can get almost everything from a great number of suppliers, most products and services have become a type of commodity. Therefore, a leader's ability to connect with the clients of the organization, provide them with extraordinary services and added value, to become their trusted advisor by building significant relationships based on trust, genuine consideration and long-term personal acquaintance – is of great importance.

Another equally important aspect is leading change.

To effectively lead change, a leader must connect with his employees at the emotional level.

Successful leaders will be the ones who defy the status quo, constantly challenging it with new concepts and ideas and recreating themselves, their staff, their department and their organization.

Questions for Mirroring and Development

Estimate to what extent are the following statements important to you at work:

1. To follow predetermined schedules.
2. To hold discussion groups in which listening and sharing are possible.
3. To take part in training or coaching programs.
4. Before setting out on a new path:
   - To have a proof of validity and research
   - To be provided with exact and concise data
   - To have clear objectives and results presented to you
5. To learn from formal presentations, as well as from sources such as data, textbooks and bibliographies.
6. To have opportunities to share emotions and display empathy and consideration for other people's needs.
7. To have good interpersonal relationships with your superiors.
8. To hold team-building activities and events for the department.

9. To put an emphasis on organization and consistency so that each process has a clear beginning, middle and end.

10. To have things predefined and accompanied by demonstrations in order to facilitate their implementation.

11. To experience learning through cooperation in small group learning projects.

12. To have progress measured in every process – before and after.

13. For the problem-solving process, to act in a constructive, methodological way.

14. To have opportunities to think outside the box and experiment, and to be given freedom to explore and discover.

15. To have opportunities to work with numbers and measurable data and to make use of services provided by experts.

16. To have opportunities to talk about vision and how to fulfill it.

EQ Land

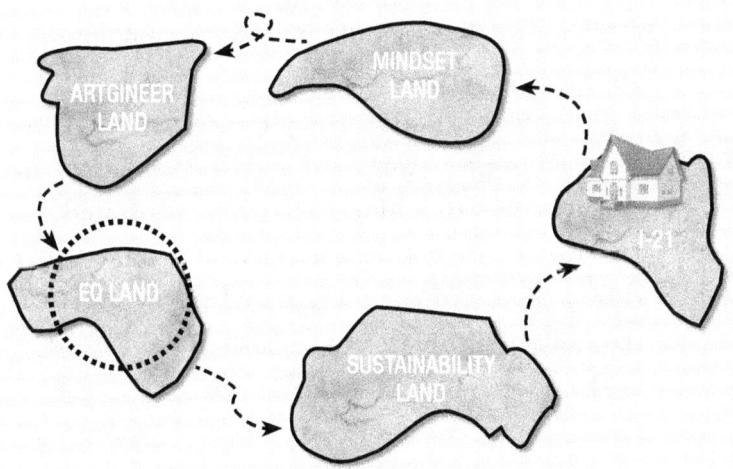

Questions for Thought and Reflection

Think about and explain to what extent you agree (or disagree) with the following statements:

1. As Advisors and Accountants, it's important that we don't leave room for emotions in our professional lives.

2. What influences our success the most is our Intelligence Quotient (IQ).

3. Emotional intelligence is an array of skills mostly related to interpersonal aspects.

4. Our professional and personal success is an outcome of our emotional intelligence.

5. It is impossible to significantly develop and improve one's emotional intelligence.

6. The concept of emotional intelligence is meaningless in the business world. It is only meaningful in professions like teaching, social work and psychology.

7. The concept of emotional intelligence pertains to the correlation between emotion and intelligence, i.e. the ability to use reason to manage emotions, and to use emotions in the thinking process.

8. A growth mindset is a necessary precondition for developing emotional intelligence.

Emotional Intelligence

"If the driving force of intelligence in twentieth-century business has been IQ, then – according to growing evidence – in the dawning twenty-first century it will be EQ, and related forms of practical and creative intelligence."

- Sawaf and Cooper

1. What is the meaning of the concept "Emotional Intelligence"?

The concept of emotional intelligence pertains to the interaction between emotion and thinking (between emotional processes and cognitive processes) and their correlation. It includes the ability to use sound judgment and reasoning when managing emotions, and the ability to use emotional considerations in decision-making processes.

A number of definitions of emotional intelligence appear in the professional literature. The following are two of the most prominent definitions:

- **Mayer and Salovey:** "...the ability to monitor one's own and others' feelings and emotions, to discriminate among them and to use this information to guide one's thinking and action." [66]

- **Reuven Bar-On:** "…an array of personal, emotional and social competencies and skills that influence one's ability to succeed in coping with environmental demands and pressures." [67]

2. What was the basis for this concept's development?

The idea at the core of the emotional intelligence concept is not a new one. Similar concepts, which were studied throughout most of the 20th century, have their historical roots as far back as the 19th century. In fact, even in Greek philosophy, as well as in humanistic psychology, one can find debates regarding the importance of our emotions, their connection to the way we think and their consequent impact on our success. Similar discussions appear in work published by Charles Darwin about the contribution of emotions (and their expression) to survival.

Even though the predominant perception in the 20th century was that cognitive intelligence is the major contributor to success, psychologist Robert Thorndike argued in 1920 for the existence and importance of social intelligence.[68] According to his definition, social intelligence includes the ability to understand the emotions, motives and behaviors of the self and others. It comprises the ability to accurately perceive the social map and to act optimally based on this information; the ability to act wisely in interpersonal relationships, to communicate and to act in synergy with another individual. Even though his studies were not accepted during his time, they served as the basis for the concept's development.

Twenty years later, David Wechsler,[69] the developer of the IQ test, argued that there are more factors or components beyond those that exist in current evaluations of intelligence. He further argued that models of intelligence would not be complete without such components, which are important to the prediction of success. As a result, Wechsler incorporated two such components that pertain to interpersonal skills in his IQ test. The recognition of a wider view of intelligence thrived when Howard Gardner presented his theory of multiple intelligences,[70] in which interpersonal intelligence and intrapersonal intelligence were included, among others. These components became the basis for the concept of emotional intelligence.

And still, emotional intelligence is a rather new field of research that has developed over the last three decades. The first researchers who dealt with it as a new field of research and used the term "Emotional Intelligence" were John Mayer, a psychology professor at the University of New Hampshire, and Peter Salovey, head of the psychology department at Yale.

By the end of the 1980s, Mayer and Salovey published the first articles on the correlation between emotion and intelligence, areas which had been studied separately until then.[71] They then continued to study the field and validate emotional intelligence as a separate form of intelligence. The interest in the area greatly increased in 1995 both as a subject of research and among the general public, following the publication of Daniel Goleman's book.[72] Later, Goleman's article on emotional intelligence at work was selected as one of HBR's *Breakthrough Ideas for Today's Business*

Agenda and as one of HBR's *10 Must Reads on Leadership*. Since then, emotional intelligence has been studied at the leading universities and a respectable number of books and doctoral theses have been published on the subject.

3. What are the components of Emotional Intelligence?

Emotional intelligence is a collection of skills related to the link between emotions, behaviors and thinking. There are various models that use different names and present slightly different lists of emotional intelligence components or scales. However, what is common to all of them is that they include awareness of one's own emotions and the emotions of others, management of emotions and relationships.

The Mayer and Salovey Model

The Mayer and Salovey[73] model for emotional intelligence is a four-branch model comprised of four hierarchically organized <u>abilities</u>:

- **Perceiving Emotions:** The ability to identify one's own emotions and the emotions of others. The ability to detect and decipher emotions in faces, pictures, voices and cultural artifacts such as art, stories or music (as well as express emotions through these). Perceiving emotions represents a basic aspect of emotional intelligence, as it makes all other processing of emotional information possible.
- **Reasoning With Emotions:** The ability to harness emotions to facilitate various cognitive activities such as thinking, problem-solving and decision-

making. The emotionally intelligent individual can capitalize fully upon their changing moods in order to best fit the task at hand.

- **Understanding Emotions:** The ability to understand emotions and emotional information, to comprehend the language of emotions, to appreciate complicated relationships between emotions and to recognize and describe how emotions evolve over time.

- **Managing Emotions:** The ability to regulate (manage or adapt) emotions in both ourselves and in others, in order to promote emotional and intellectual growth. The emotionally intelligent person can harness emotions, including negative ones, and manage them to achieve intended goals.

The Daniel Goleman Model

Other models expanded the definition of emotional intelligence to include abilities and skills that have behavioral aspects, which are also related to effective functioning. Focusing on the competencies and skills that drive leadership performance, psychologist Daniel Goleman outlined five major components:

- **Self-awareness:** The ability to recognize and understand personal moods, emotions and drives, as well as their influence on others; the ability to realistically evaluate our strengths and weaknesses; the ability to use these understandings when making decisions and solving problems.

- **Self-regulation:** The ability to manage, control and redirect our emotions (especially disruptive ones and impulses) so that they assist us in achieving our goals, rather than interrupt us. The ability to adapt to changing circumstances and properly recover from emotional distress.

- **Motivation:** The ability to be driven to achieve for the sake of achievement. The strength that comes from an internal vision that guides us toward objectives that go beyond external rewards (such as money or status). The ability to initiate, take advantage of opportunities and aspire to constant improvement, even in the face of barriers and frustrations.

- **Empathy:** The ability to understand the emotions and viewpoints of others, nurturing harmony and attuning to a wide variety of individuals. The ability to respond to people according to their emotional reactions and consider their feelings when making decisions.

- **Social skills:** The ability to manage relationships in order to move people in the desired direction. The ability to properly handle the emotions involved in relationships and accurately interpret social situations and networks; the ability to conduct smooth interactions; the use of these skills to guide, negotiate, cooperate and work in teams.

The Reuven Bar-On Model

Reuven Bar-On, a clinical and organizational psychologist, devoted over 25 years to emotional intelligence research. Bar-On defined emotional intelligence as follows: "A multi-factorial array of interrelated emotional and social competencies, skills and facilitators that influence one's ability to recognize, understand and manage emotions, to relate with others, to adapt to change and solve problems of a personal and interpersonal nature, and to efficiently cope with daily demands, challenges and pressures."

As is evident from this definition, emotional intelligence includes many aspects of life. It is therefore not only necessary for efficient and effective functioning, but also critical for success in life and at work.

The model developed by Bar-On[74] describes emotional intelligence through five composite scales composed of a total of 15 subscales.

- **The Intra-Personal Component:** One's ability to be aware of their emotions, to understand them and to express them. It includes the subscales of Self-Regard, Emotional Self-Awareness, Assertiveness, Independence and Self-Actualization.

- **The Inter-Personal Component:** One's ability to be aware of the emotions of others, to understand and reflect them, to attend to others or assist them and to have good relationships. It includes the subscales of Empathy, Social Responsibility and Interpersonal Relationship.

- **Adaptability:** One's ability to adapt their emotions, thoughts and behavior to changing conditions and situations, and to cope with changes. It includes the subscales of Reality Testing, Flexibility and Problem Solving.

- **Stress Management:** One's ability to cope with their feelings in stressful situations so that they act in one's favor and not against him. It includes the subscales of Stress Tolerance and Impulse Control.

- **General Mood:** One's ability to be positive and to motivate oneself. It includes the subscales of Optimism and Happiness.

4. How can we measure Emotional Intelligence?

Emotional intelligence is a scientific concept that is measurable and can be developed. There are a number of tools for measuring and evaluating emotional intelligence. Among others:

MSCEIT: Together with David Caruso, Mayer and Salovey composed the first emotional intelligence test, which is referred to as a "multi-factor measurement for the evaluation of emotional intelligence" – a descendant of a previous test they had created (the MEIS). The Mayer-Salovey-Caruso Emotional Intelligence Test is an ability measure that is based on a variety of tasks, which is designed to examine the four components of the Mayer and Salovey model.[75]

ECI: Daniel Goleman and Richard Boyatzis formulated the Emotional Competence Inventory test, which examines the central aspects of Goleman's model. It also integrates self-report with the reports of others who are familiar with the subject of the evaluation (360-degree evaluation, also known as Multi-Rater Feedback). This tool is intended for the business sector and especially for management and leadership positions.[76]

EQ-i: A significant part of Bar-On's work focused on developing a measurement tool, the Emotional Quotient Inventory, which is considered a leading self-report measure of emotional intelligence. The test renders scores for the 15 subscales of the Bar-On model, the five composite scales and the total EQ score. In addition, based on built-in validity indices, the test includes a correction factor that reduces potential bias and makes the test more accurate.[77]

EQ-i 2.0: This 2011 revision of the EQ-i includes some new features. It reflects a continued evolution of the concept of emotional intelligence and puts a greater emphasis on effectiveness in the workplace and on leadership in particular. The subscales are redefined with less overlap and all composite scales have 3 sub-scales. One major new feature is the distinction between Self-Perception and Self-Expression, which includes the new subscale of Emotional Expression. Decision Making is another new composite scale, which addresses the way in which we use emotional information in the decision making process.

5. How is Emotional Intelligence related to the business world?

Many people will argue that in order to succeed in the business world, one must not mix emotions and business. In fact, the opposite is true. A growing number of studies indicate that the intelligent use of emotions is highly necessary to identify problems and opportunities and to make better decisions.

Over 30 years ago, researchers studying effectiveness in organizations expressed concern over the fact that the widely used assessments were not good predictors of an individual's life and work success. One of the most prominent researchers, David McClelland of Harvard, believed that the ability to predict success based on academic achievements, technical skills and an impressive résumé, can be as low as 20%.

In 1973, McClelland published a revolutionary article entitled *Testing for Competence Rather than Intelligence*,[78] an article which strongly promoted the creation of a new approach to identifying excellent employees. McClelland argues that if an organization wished to hire or promote the best individual for a certain job, an executive job, for instance, it must ignore the accepted metrics.

The modern work environment and its centrality in our everyday lives create a broad range of emotions. The ability to successfully manage our emotional world and to act out of choice and out of a value system is crucial for success in the workplace.

Studies at various organizations have confirmed the contribution of emotional intelligence to outcomes such as employee effectiveness and productivity, through measurable operational indicators such as execution and income levels, relationships and teamwork, commitment to the workplace, stress tolerance and management skills of executives.[79]

For instance:

- In interviews with 2,000,000 employees at 700 American companies, it was found that what determined both the amount of time invested by employees and their productivity was the quality of the relationship between the employees and their superiors. It appeared that people were joining companies, but leaving managers.

- At American Express, business consultants who attended a workshop to improve their emotional intelligence increased their sales by 18.1% in comparison with a control group, which increased its sales by only 6.2%. This is an annual profit of around USD 200 million.

- At a nationwide insurance firm, it was found that insurance agents who received low scores in emotional intelligence skills such as self-confidence, initiative and empathy, sold an average amount of USD 54,000 in premiums. Those who achieved high scores, in at least five emotional intelligence subscales, sold policies with premiums of USD 114,000.

- A study focusing on a large number of professions found that salespersons endowed with high emotional intelligence were 12 times as productive as the ones at the bottom.

All over the world, a growing number of organizations now understand the business significance of recruiting employees with high emotional intelligence and of developing emotional intelligence in their existing employees. If in the past, they would state that **the human resource** is the most important asset of an organization, today they emphasize the higher importance of **the right human resource**.

Emotional intelligence is especially critical for executive (leadership) positions. Executives and leaders must make many decisions, interact with a wide variety of individuals, communicate ideas, connect people to a vision and inspire people to follow them. They must function in a changing environment, under high stress, and they must lead their employees and the entire organization to success. Inter-personal and intra-personal skills are highly important in these tasks. An executive who is aware of his emotions will be able to successfully manage and regulate them through hard times. He will be capable of understanding, motivating and connecting with others.

6. What characterizes executives with high Emotional Intelligence?

Executives with high emotional intelligence are aware of their emotions and their thoughts in various situations. They have a better understanding of their emotions and can manage them successfully. They can also demonstrate self-regulation, acting by choice rather than by emotional hijacking (or *Amygdala hijacking*, a term coined by Daniel Goleman to describe emotions that inhibit a person from viewing a situation realistically).

Their awareness of their values, purpose and knowledge enables them to set challenging yet realistic objectives and strive to attain them. They have a high sense of self-actualization and a growth mindset. They strive for constant learning and development and are not afraid to take risks and step out of their comfort zone. Their ability to clearly express their opinions and needs enables them to achieve their objectives. They are flexible and adapt easily to changes; they know how to act, even in stressful situations, how to remain optimistic and happy and how to communicate these feelings to their employees. They understand the emotions of others (employees, colleagues and superiors), recognize their needs, provide them with an appropriate response and build positive and productive relationships. They create a shared vision and successfully motivate others to join in.

Many studies related to emotional intelligence have been conducted among executives. In a study by Richard Boyatzis,[80] which included over 200 executives at various levels in 12 organizations, it was shown that 14 out of the 16 skills that differentiate excellent executives from their mediocre colleagues were emotional skills. Among those were accurate self-evaluation, assertiveness, emotional self-control and organizational awareness.

In another study conducted by Hay and McBer, which included hundreds of senior executives from 15 global companies such as PepsiCo, Volvo and IBM, emotional skills were found to be a crucial factor in differentiating between mediocre leaders and the best leaders.[81] The latter demonstrated significantly higher levels of emotional skills such as team leadership, political awareness, assertiveness and the drive to achieve.

McClelland surveyed data from more than 30 different organizations about management positions in various professions such as banking, sales and medicine.[82] The survey pointed to the fact that a wide variety of emotional skills (and a narrow range of intellectual skills) distinguished between excellent executives and mediocre ones. The most significant emotional abilities were found to be the drive to achieve (motivation), adaptability, the development of others, influencing others, assertiveness and leadership. Meanwhile, the most significant intellectual ability was found to be analytical thinking.[83]

7. What are the characteristics of executives with low Emotional Intelligence?

Executives with low emotional intelligence tend to focus on tasks rather than on individuals. They tend neither to internalize nor tune in to their own emotions. Low self-awareness may lead them to be unaware of the emotions they bring to the workplace and how they react and communicate.

These executives might snap at their employees when they are upset, hurt their feelings and hinder their sense of security. Generally, they tend to be unaware of the feelings and needs of the individuals around them and attach little significance to them.

These factors compromise their ability to create a sense of belonging, loyalty and commitment amongst their employees and to inspire them to follow their lead. They also compromise their ability to create the positive and joyful atmosphere that is vital for satisfaction in the workplace. They find it difficult to leave their comfort zone and effectively lead change, and will eventually become irrelevant in most situations. These are executives that no one wants to work with.

8. Can Emotional Intelligence be developed?

Emotional intelligence develops gradually from a young age until early adulthood.[84] Even so, it is possible to develop and improve it at any stage and age through learning and training. Such processes deal with identification of the individual's strengths and challenges and with the focused development of skills that require improvement. These processes require will and personal engagement as well as a commitment to invest time and effort.

Studies dealing with the evaluation of such processes in organizations point to an increase in emotional intelligence (as measured by emotional intelligence tests), as well as in work effectiveness.

9. Which EI-based processes are performed by organizations?

Researchers refer to team, group and even organizational emotional intelligence. Steven Stein defines organizational emotional intelligence as the ability of an organization to reach high achievements while devoting attention to all the parties involved.[85] Many companies (such as Johnson & Johnson, Motorola, HP and American Express) conduct training and workshops aimed at improving emotional intelligence skills of employees, as a means to increase organizational effectiveness and profits.

Such processes are usually adapted to the particular organization and its needs. They first include an extensive assessment of the organization's needs, the challenges it faces and its readiness for change.

The implementation stage commonly includes strategic organizational changes that are conveyed through the development programs in a variety of ways such as lectures, workshops and personal development for managers and employees.

The implementation of such processes should involve the mobilization of management and the creation of a leading team. They should also include proper incentives in order to generate motivation for the change at the personal and organizational levels.

Such a process should include a long-term sustainability approach to assert the persistence of the change, including process evaluation and the examination of its effectiveness and possible improvements.

10. How is Emotional Intelligence related to success in the 21st century?

Keller & Price, two senior consultants at McKinsey, recently published a ground-breaking book entitled *Beyond Performances*.[86] Based on hundreds of studies, they concluded that an organization that wishes to excel in the 21st century must look beyond the business performance and put an emphasis on organizational health.

Organizational health is the organization's ability to renew itself faster than the competition in order to maintain outstanding performance over time. The writers note nine central factors through which organizations create the organizational health necessary for success in the 21st century. Among others, they mention the following factors:

- **Orientation:** A clear and significant sense among all the employees in the organization of where the organization is heading to and how it will get there.
- **Leadership:** The extent to which leaders motivate the organization's employees.
- **Motivation:** The existence of enthusiasm that inspires individuals to make their best effort and give their best performance in order to accomplish tasks and achieve goals.
- **External orientation:** The quality of the relationships with clients, providers, partners and other stakeholders, in order to generate value.
- **Innovation and learning:** The quality and flow of new ideas – the organization's ability to adapt and reshape itself when necessary.

In order to create the required organizational health, organizations, will undoubtedly have to realize that their leaders need to possess high emotional intelligence, as it is the basis for all the factors mentioned by Keller and Price.

Questions for Mirroring and Development

1. As a leader, is it important for you to express your emotions? If so, how do you express them? In what contexts?

2. Think of a situation in which you were in a good mood at work. How did your mood influence your work? How did it affect your environment?

3. To what extent would you describe yourself as flexible in your thinking and behavior?

4. To what extent would you describe yourself as an individual who often gets what he wants? How do you do it?

5. In your mind, is it important to integrate emotions into thinking and decision-making processes? Think of an example in which you did so to good effect.

6. Try to recall a situation in which you were decisive and resolute at work. What was the issue about? Why were you resolute in this case? What did you say? How did you say it? What did others think?

7. Can you normally detect what other people are feeling? If so, does it help you to perform better? How?

8. As a leader, are relationships with other individuals in the organization highly significant to you?

9. To what extent would you describe yourself as someone who functions well under pressure?

10. Can you think of a case in which you formed an opinion about someone that ran counter to others' opinion, and you turned out to be right?

11. To what extent would you say that you understand organizational politics?

12. Think of a case or a time period in which you had to adapt to change. How did you feel about the change? How did you adapt?

13. Would you describe yourself as an optimistic individual? How do you know?

14. To what extent are happiness and satisfaction important to you?

15. If you could add three things to your life that would make you happier, what would they be?

Sustainability Land

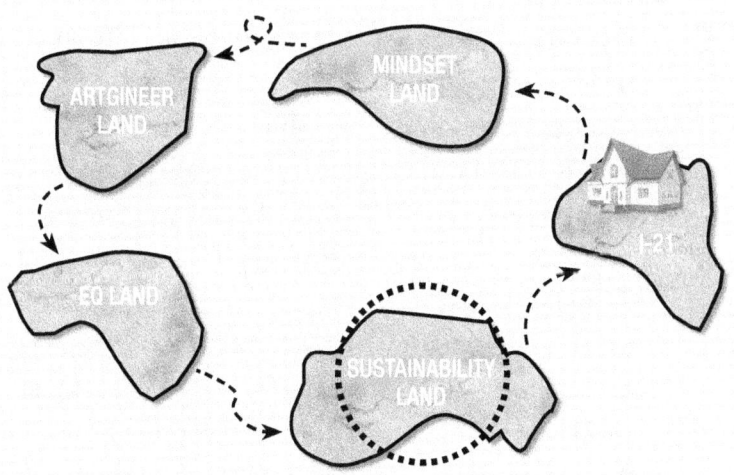

Questions for Thought and Reflection

Think about and explain to what extent you agree (or disagree) with the following statements:

1. The sense of significance we find at work contributes substantially to our sense of motivation and to that of our subordinates.

2. The framework through which we choose to view and process the world around us affects personal and professional outcomes in our lives.

3. Optimistic people are generally more successful than pessimistic people.

4. People with strong social networks and good mentors progress faster, earn more and are more satisfied with their careers, because of their ability to forge significant relationships.

5. In order to be meaningful in an organization it is important to take risks and state your opinion clearly and unambiguously, even if it deviates from the majority opinion.

6. In order to progress, it is important for leaders to assume full responsibility for their career development and professional development.

7. Only leaders who know how to take good emotional, physical and cognitive care of themselves will succeed over time.

Sustainability

1. What is the meaning of the term "Centered Leadership"?

Centered Leadership is a combination of five dimensions or practices, proven to be the most important for self-actualization and success in a changing, complex and dynamic reality. The model focuses on intellectual, physical, emotional and mental strengths. These strengths lead executives to personal success and high levels of professional achievements. This success inspires others and makes them want to follow their lead. It should be noted that this is not a leadership model, but rather a collection of practices that can assist people in leading themselves and others and achieving greater success in the dynamic and complex world of the 21st century.

2. Who created the model and what is it based on?

The centered leadership model is the product of a five-year study in which 100 leading women executives participated through in-depth interviews and 2,000 additional women executives participated through surveys. These included renowned CEOs in the business world, scientists, artists and executives at government offices.

Barsh and Cranston, two senior consultants at McKinsey, tried to examine what led these executives to success.[87] From the results of their interviews, they extracted and refined an impressive model referred to as the Centered Leadership model. This model describes the characteristics of executives who will be able to successfully lead in a changing, hyper-competitive and increasingly complex world.

3. Is this model only applicable to women executives?

Even though the model was created based on a study of leading women, it is undoubtedly valid for male executives as well. As evidence, the model was adopted by two researchers from McKinsey, Keller and Price, in their book *Beyond Performances*.[88] Discussing the issue of leadership, the writers follow the centered leadership model and describe its contribution to the success of leaders, regardless of gender.

The book deals with the ways to achieve business and organizational excellence in a reality that is very different from that of the 20th century. Keller and Price present an extensive model based on in-depth interviews and the analysis of hundreds of studies conducted at organizations. They conclude that in the complex and uncertain reality of our time, many organizations will disappear because they are incapable of managing effective change processes. Only organizations that are capable of **integrating performance, focus and organizational health** will succeed over time. This remains true regardless of the gender of the organization's managers.

4. What are the components of the model?

The model is composed of five dimensions whose integration provides leaders with the endurance and emotional abilities required for continuous self-improvement, as well as for improving the organization they work in.

When the five dimensions of centered leadership are put together, they enable people to achieve their goals in life and at work through a clear sense of purpose, belonging, resilience and control. Centered leaders feel they can lead constant changes in their organization and make the most of any challenge or opportunity.

A survey conducted by McKinsey among 1,147 senior executives found that executives who noted that they were characterized by four or five of these dimensions had high levels of passion for work, were effective leaders and were satisfied with their lives. It was also found that the five dimensions reinforced one another.

These are the five dimensions and their characteristics:

Meaning: Discovering who we are and what we were meant to do.

Typically, leaders and professionals who rank high on this dimension feel highly committed to their work and strive to achieve their goals out of passion and enthusiasm. They have a deep emotional connection to their field of expertise. They are aware of their strengths, use them and inspire others to act likewise. In contrast, leaders who lack a sense of meaning will live their life from one weekend to the next. It was also found that sense of meaning is closely correlated with happiness and energy, and therefore leaders with a strong sense of meaning seem to work effortlessly and seem to find nothing to be too difficult for them.

In fact, this dimension's contribution to general satisfaction with life is five times higher than that of the other dimensions. The explanation is simple: a sense of meaning makes us participate in activities we enjoy and use our strengths. We experience a sense of accomplishment, and our work, even if it is difficult and challenging, invokes energy instead of draining it. The contribution of a sense of meaning to happiness is widely supported by research. In one of the most prominent studies, Sonja Lyubomirsky noted that finding meaning is the safest way to increase an individual's level of happiness in the long run.[89]

In addition to the positive implications of the meaning dimension at the personal level, it also has an organizational contribution: when leaders find meaning and feel connected to activities related to their goals, they generate positive energy around them and inspire others. The sense of meaning experienced by the staff increases their motivation and effectiveness in a way that cannot be achieved through formal incentives or a sanction system. Thus, the effect of meaning is cyclic: as leaders contribute to a cause larger than themselves (to other individuals in the organization or to the organization itself), their sense of meaning grows stronger and they become more inspiring to others.

Positive framing: Finding opportunities in difficulties, seeing difficult problems in a way that encourages creative solutions and innovation.

Positive framing plays a role in almost every aspect of one's professional life, regardless of their field of specialization – when facing clients, colleagues, superiors or subordinates, as well as when leading organizational processes.

The framing through which we choose to view and interpret the world influences our personal and professional achievements. It is important to note that "positive framing" does not mean putting on a pair of rose-colored glasses, but rather the ability to see the facts as they are and still emphasize the positive. Leaders who positively frame their reality can lead their teams towards feelings of capability and ability, rather than submission and helplessness.

Pessimistic people tend to see negative situations as permanent, broad ranging and self-derived. This limits their thinking, prevents them from bringing forth strategic concepts and drains their energies. Meanwhile, optimistic people see negative situations as temporary, distinct and external. This enables them to see the situation with greater objectivity and respond quickly.

Optimistic individuals, who naturally choose to focus on the opportunities presented in every situation, have higher success rates in comparison with pessimistic individuals, who focus on the dangers and threats. Though we are not all born optimistic, studies do indicate that our observation of life is only half innate. Studies presented by Seligman in his book *Learned Optimism*[90] indicate that people can acquire tools that are deployed automatically by optimistic individuals when they view situations. Optimism, whether natured or nurtured, underlies leaders' ability to be flexible and to recuperate: to take blows, evaluate their implications and respond in an appropriate and effective manner.

However, it is important to maintain a balance between optimism and a fair sense of perspective and reality testing, as positive framing cannot be achieved in all situations and at all times.

Connecting with others: Being part of a group, growing, developing and achieving together.

This dimension relates to a leader's ability to create meaningful relationships with people of different groups. Studies indicate that people who have strong social networks and good mentors tend to progress faster, earn more and be more satisfied with their careers. This means that creating meaningful relationships is part of a leader's everyday job.

Successful leaders build complex networks of connections, which increase their personal influence and accelerate their development, thanks to the variety of ideas and the experience they are exposed to through these connections. As to such a network of influential people, it isn't restricted to the list of the organization's senior executive. It also includes lower rank key employees, who are not necessarily managers. Exposure to lower rank employees and the benefits of this exposure, are what Jack Walsh terms "reverse mentoring."

As a rule, relationships are essential to both our emotional well-being and success. People who invest in their relationships, find that others are willing to assist them and to support their wishes, thus making them more successful as leaders.

Leaders who build such relationships, namely who develop a network of relations with other professionals can use them in a way that assists them to make better and more professional decisions. They consult with the relevant experts in different fields, in order to widen their perspective and deepen their knowledge. They have an effective and productive relationship with their professional relations and use them to reach meaningful insights. Also, as they have great respect for mentoring processes, they serve as exceptional mentors for young employees. In their book *Exceptional Leadership*,[91] Garman and Dye claim that one of the key competencies of exceptional leaders is the ability to serve as mentors for professionals who are just starting out.

Engaging: Finding our voice, showing courage, sticking to our opinions and taking advantage of opportunities in spite of the risks

Engagement is closely related to taking risks; it means being proactive and assuming responsibility for taking action. It means understanding that we are responsible for our organizational environment and have the ability to influence it, as opposed to being passive and feeling that nothing is in our control. Engagement is not the same as positive framing. While positive framing allows us to see opportunities, engagement provides us with the courage to try: to set our fears aside and make use of the opportunities we have identified.

Engaged leaders feel a sense of capability, act with determination and strive to achieve their goals. They take risks and express their opinions and desires clearly and unequivocally, even if they differ from the majority opinion. They are not afraid to be critical of opinion leaders or of professional literature and studies. They understand that in a constantly changing reality, one has to ask the right questions in order to avoid mistakes. They also take full responsibility for their career development and professional development. Generally, these are leaders who are willing to invest much effort in order to build their own personal and professional value proposition – a value proposition that is optimal for facing the challenges of an ever-changing world. Such leaders are willing to leave their fancy offices and assist in solving necessary operational issues.

Energizing: Methodically investing in physical, mental and emotional energy and creating the actions and habits necessary to stimulate energy in other individuals

Everyone has a limited amount of energy - from the CEO in his fancy office to the most junior employee. The challenging reality in which we live demands that we exert massive amounts of energy on a daily basis. Constant improvement requires enthusiasm and commitment from many individuals within the organization. For this to be possible, leaders must know how to preserve their own energy and that of others, and to avoid the exhaustion of their resources.

It is well known that executives and senior employees work hard and that a significant part of them are unable to achieve a balance between their jobs and their lives outside of work. However, one's awareness of the fact that he must find this balance as a leader – both for himself and for his employees can lead him to better life habits.

Individuals who are occupied with things they are good at and love to do are also more likely to maintain high energy levels. When we use our core skills – our strengths – to overcome challenges and achieve goals, we experience a mental state in which our work is perceived as effortless. As a result, we have better output, higher productivity and greater satisfaction from our work. This is the mental state that psychologist Mihaly Csikszentmihalyi defines as "flow".[92]

How can we experience flow? Typically, by doing a job that we love and is within our abilities. Thus, when facing challenging objectives that involve using our skills, we can focus on the task at hand and devote our best efforts to it while requiring less energy to do so.

However, it is important to remember that sometimes, even when we are focused on the task at hand and feel capable and motivated, we may still fail. In general, our ability to easily recover from failure attests to our resilience and adaptability. This is a leadership quality that is essential in order to sustain a constant process of improvement. But our ability to recover and regroup our energies is dependent on the four other dimensions of the centered leadership model – awareness of what is significant to us (the passions and strengths that can help us succeed); maintaining a positive point of view; using our social networks; and courageous engagement and willingness to face risks head on. One of the most important roles of leaders is to create high levels of positive energy in their teams. Only leaders who can protect their own well-being over time will be able to do so effectively.

5. Which Centered Leadership related processes are performed by organizations?

Organizations perform various processes to strengthen the five dimensions of the centered leadership model, even if they are unaware of it. For instance, the implementation of programs related to social responsibility has to do with a sense of organizational meaning. So does the embedding of a vision and values. Various training programs, such as team-building and monitoring processes, are related to the dimension of connecting with others and to effective communication. Attempts to build Work-Life Balance programs are related to the dimension of energy creation.

The most challenging dimension, which many organizations still find hard to handle, is the dimension of engagement, as fewer employees and executives feel a personal connection or commitment to the organizations in which they work. Thus, they may not assume full responsibility for various processes in the organization.

6. How is the Centered Leadership model related to the 21st century?

Though the five dimensions of the centered leadership model have always been important to the success of executives, nowadays the dynamic, demanding, complex and competitive reality leads many executives to reach the limits of their abilities. This is why each of the dimensions, and all of them combined, are important for the survival and success of executives and organizations.

Adopting the centered leadership model changes the point of view of executives and makes them focus on their personal responsibility for shaping their own future. If in the 20th century executives were more passive and would often tell themselves that "the organization is going to worry about my career plan" or "the organization is going to notify me of my responsibilities" and so on, the centered leadership model places the brunt of the responsibility on the shoulders of the executive aspiring to lead. Leaders who know how to be proactive and use these five dimensions will continue to succeed over time; those who do not – will disappear.

When it comes to leading change processes, an executive who sets out on this task devoid of energy is guaranteed not to make it through the change effectively. Leaders who know how to take care of themselves and their energy levels will undoubtedly succeed in managing others in the raging white waters.

7. Can the various dimensions of the model be developed?

Certainly. Anyone who wishes to develop these dimensions can do so. The dimensions described above are based on emotional intelligence skills. This is why an executive with high capabilities within relevant emotional intelligence skills can turn any dimension into an action plan and start developing it. An executive who lacks these skills must first develop the relevant "muscles" and only then set a plan for action.

For instance, if a manager has good interpersonal skills, he or she should build a program to strengthen and preserve their social network inside and outside the organization – decide who the most significant individuals for the process are and what they are going to do with regard to each of them (sending e-mails, having lunch, providing assistance, planning a shared project, etc.). Later on, they can connect with a senior manager and ask them to serve as their mentor.

When it comes to strategic clients, he should set up a program that aims at becoming their trusted advisor: building a close relationship based on trust and long-term commitment.

Another example has to do with involvement and responsibility. If executives have a strong command of the skills of independence, assertiveness and self-evaluation and these do not require development, they can identify meaningful issues in the organization that are in need of improvement and take responsibility for them. Often, these are processes that no one in the organization is willing to take on, and they present an opportunity for such executives.

Later on, in important meetings, they can consciously decide which significant messages they want to communicate, and phrase them clearly. They can use a sympathetic and empathic description of their opinions and ideas, even when they are different from the ideas of others. An interesting paradox is that even though most people do not like to hear opinions different from their own, most of them can appreciate such opinions when they are expressed properly and reliably by individuals who are perceived as trustworthy and responsible, who know where to lead the team and who are capable of leading it.

Questions for Mirroring and Development

1. Go over the descriptions of each dimension of the Centered Leadership model and describe - in what ways are they related to organizational and personal sustainability? In what ways is organizational sustainability related to leadership in general?
2. Do you know why you have chosen your profession?
3. Have you ever asked yourself, "Is this what I want to keep on doing?" and answered "Yes!"?
4. Are you doing a job that brings out your strengths?
5. Do you have a sense of purpose in your job?
6. What are the characteristics that set apart exceptional leaders?
7. To what extent do you think that leadership is an innate capability?
8. Do you invest worthy efforts in order to nurture and maintain your social network?
9. Do you have a mentor with whom you can consult and who cares about your development?
10. Do you provide added value to the individuals around you (subordinates, colleagues, superiors, clients)?
11. Do you take full responsibility for your career development?
12. Are you aware of your own voice and do you make it heard?
13. Have you achieved most of your ambitions thus far?
14. Are you capable of balancing your work and your personal life? Are you actually doing so?

15. Are there enough things in your life that give you pleasure?

16. Are you getting enough sleep, eating healthy food and exercising?

17. Are you spending enough time with people who "charge you with energy"?

18. Do you celebrate personal and organizational success?

Sources

[1] Martin Reeves and Lisanne Pueschel, *Die Another Day: What Leaders Can Do About the Shrinking Life Expectancy of Corporations*, BCG Perspectives, The Boston Consulting Group, July 2015.

[2] Daniel Pink, *A Whole New Mind: Why Right-Brainers Will Rule the Future*, Riverhead Trade, 2006.

[3] Steve Tappin and Andrew Cave, *The Secrets of CEOs: 150 Global Chief Executives Lift the Lid on Business, Life and Leadership*, Nicholas Brealey Publishing, 2008.

[4] Steve Tappin and Andrew Cave, *The NEW Secrets of CEOs: 200 Global Chief Executives on Leading*, Nicholas Brealey Publishing, 2010.

[5] Rosabeth Moss Kanter, *SuperCorp: How Vanguard Companies Create Innovation, Profits, Growth, and Social Good*, Crown Business, 2009.

[6] John Veihmeyer, Chairman, KPMG International, in the forward notes to '*Now or Never: the 2016 Global CEO Outlook*,' KPMG International, 2016.

[7] Jane McCormick, Global Head of Tax, KPMG International, in 'Now or Never: the 2016 Global CEO Outlook,' KPMG International, 2016.

[8] Daniel Pink, *A Whole New Mind: Why Right-Brainers Will Rule the Future*, Riverhead Trade, 2006.

[9] The Center for Creative Leadership (CCL®) is a global provider of executive education that develops better leaders through its exclusive focus on leadership education and research.

[10] Carol Dweck, *Mindset: The New Psychology of Success*, Ballantine Books, 2007.

[11] Jerome Groopman, *How Doctors Think*, Houghton Mifflin, 2007.

[12] Andrew N. Garman and Carson F. Dye, *Exceptional Leadership: 16 Critical Competencies for Healthcare Executives*, Second Edition (ACHE Management Series), Health Administration Press, 2006.

[13] Brown, Brené, *Daring Greatly: How the Courage to Be Vulnerable Transforms the Way We Live*, Love, Parent, and Lead, Center Point Large Print, 2013.

[14] Theodore Roosevelt, Excerpt from the speech "Citizenship In A Republic" delivered at the Sorbonne, in Paris, France on 23 April, 1910.

[15] Howard Gardner, *Frames of Mind: The Theory of Multiple Intelligences*, Basic Book, 1983.

[16] Robert Sternberg, *Successful Intelligence: How Practical and Creative Intelligence Determine Success in Life*, Plume, 1997.

[17] See a more realistic version in: Bob Cook, *The Reality Behind the Myth of the Coach Who Cut Michael Jordan*, Forbes, 2012, Jan 10 (http://www.forbes.com/sites/bobcook/2012/01/10/the-reality-behind-the-myth-of-the-coach-who-cut-michael-jordan-in-high-school).

[18] Malcolm Gladwell, *Outliers*, Little, Brown, and Company, 2008.

[19] Angela Duckworth, *Grit: The Power of Passion and Perseverance*, Scribner, 2016.

[20] Ibid. 10 (Dweck).

[21] John P. Kotter, *Leading Change: An Action Plan from the World's Foremost Expert on Business Leadership*, Harvard Business Press, 1996.

[22] Francesca Gino and Bradley Staats, *Why Organizations Don't Learn*, Harvard Business Review, Nov. 2017

[23] Ned Herrmann, The Whole Brain Business Book: Unlocking the Power of *Whole* Brain Thinking in Organizations and Individuals, McGraw-Hill, 1996.

[24] Susie Weller, *Meet the Four Thinking Styles: Which One Best Describes You?* (adapted from Herrmann International, see www.hbdi.com).

[25] Brian Peccarelli, *The Robot-Accountants Are Coming*, CFO.com, May 2016.

[26] Eric Almquist, Mitchell Leiman, Darrell Rigby and Alex Roth, *Taking the Measure of Your Innovation Performance*, Bain & Company, May 08, 2013.

[27] Richard Florida, *The Rise of the Creative Class: And How It's Transforming Work, Leisure, Community, and Everyday Life*, Basic Books, 2003.

[28] John Hagel, John Seely Brown, Alok Ranjan and Daniel Byler, *Passion at work: Cultivating worker passion as a cornerstone of talent development*, Deloitte University Press, 2014.

[29] Adapted from a white paper by Michael Morgan and Ann Nehdi titled 'Know Change or No Change Will Happen' (the white paper is available on the Herrmann International Website at www.hbdi.com).

[30] *Executing Together: The Clear Choice, Board and Council Retreat - Execution Guidebook*, KPMG LLP, 2015

[31] Carol Dweck and Kathleen Hogan, *How Microsoft Uses a Growth Mindset to Develop Leaders*, Harvard Business Review, Oct. 2016.

[32] Joey Havens, *Becoming the Firm of the Future*, AICPA, American Institute of CPAs, 2014.

[33] Klaus Schwab, *Shaping the Fourth Industrial Revolution*, World Economic Forum, 2018.

[34] The Grant and Glueck study, *The Harvard Study of Adult Development*, www.adultdevelopmentstudy.org

[35] See Robert Waldinger's TED talk, *What Makes a Good Life? Lessons from the Longest Study on Happiness*, 2015.

[36] *Minister for Loneliness Appointed to Continue Jo Cox's Work*, www.bbc.com, 17 January 2018.

[37] Spencer Johnson, *Who Moved My Cheese*, Vermilion, 1999.

[38] Reuven Bar-On, *The Bar-On Emotional Quotient Inventory (EQ-i): Technical Manual*, Multi-Health Systems, 1997.

[39] Peter Salovey and John D. Mayer, "*Emotional Intelligence*," in Imagination, Cognition and Personality 9 (3), 1989, pp. 185–211.

[40] Daniel Goleman, *Emotional Intelligence: Why it Can Matter More than IQ*, Bantam Books, 1995.

[41] Moshe Zeidner, Gerald Matthews, Richard D. Roberts, *What We Know about Emotional Intelligence: How It Affects Learning, Work, Relationships, and Our Mental Health*, A Bradford Book, 2012.

[42] Roberts, R.D., Zeidner, M., & Matthews, G. (2001). *Does emotional intelligence meet traditional standards for an intelligence? Some new data and conclusions.* Emotion, 1, pp. 196–231.

[43] Larry Bossidy and Ram Charan, *Execution: The Discipline of Getting Things Done*, Random House Business Books, 2002.

[44] Ibid. 38 (Bar-On).

[45] KPMG UK CEO Outlook 2017, *Disrupt and grow* (June 2017).

[46] Julian Birkinshaw and Martine Haas, *Increase Your Return on Failure*, Harvard Business Review, May 2016, pp. 88–93.

[47] See on YouTube - *Business Leadership for the 21st Century* (Davos Annual Meeting 2010) and *The Future of Enterprise* (Davos Annual Meeting 2011), World Economic Forum.

[48] Joanna Barsh, Susie Cranston and Geoffrey Lewis, *How Remarkable Women Lead: The Breakthrough Model for Work and Life,* Crown, 2009.

[49] Scott Keller and Colin Price, *Beyond Performance: How Great Organizations Build Ultimate Competitive Advantage,* John Wiley and Sons, 2011.

[50] Barsh, J. & De Smet, A., *Centered leadership through the crisis: McKinsey survey results*, McKinsey Quarterly, October 2009.

[51] Barsh, J., Mogelof, J. & Webb, C., *The value of centered leadership: McKinsey Global Survey Results*, McKinsey & Company, New York, 2010.

[52] Csikszentmihalyi, M., *Flow: The Psychology of Optimal Experience*, New York: Harper and Row, 1990.

[53] *Becoming The Clear Choice*, International Partners Conference, KPMG International Cooperative, Prague, Sep. 2016

[54] Ibid. 10 (Dweck).

[55] Ibid. 10 (Dweck).

[56] Ibid. 21 (Kotter).

[57] John P. Kotter, *A Sense of Urgency*, Harvard Business School

Publishing, 2008.

[58] Harvard Business Review Staff, *How Companies Can Profit from a "Growth Mindset"*, Harvard Business Review, November 2014, pp. 28-32.

[59] Gary Hamel and C. K. Prahalad, *Competing for the Future*, Harvard Business Review 1996.

[60] Howard Gardner, *Changing Minds: The Art and Science of Changing Our Own and Other People's Minds*, Harvard Business School, 2004

[61] Ibid. 23 (Herrmann).

[62] Herrmann Brain Dominance Instrument. In Wikipedia: The Free Encyclopedia. Wikimedia Foundation Inc. Encyclopedia on-line. Retrieved 2 February 2015. Available from http:// en.wikipedia.org/wiki/Herrmann_Brain_Dominance_ Instrument.

[63] HBDI: Herrmann Brain Dominance Instrument

[64] Daniel H. Pink, *Drive: The Surprising Truth About What Motivates Us*, Penguin Group US, 2009.

[65] Gary Hamel, *The Future of Management*, Harvard Business Review Press, 1997.

[66] Mayer, J. D., & Salovey, P., *"What is emotional intelligence?"* - in Peter Salovey and David Sluyter (eds.), *Emotional Development and Emotional Intelligence: Educational Implications*, Basic Books, 1997, pp. 3-31.

[67] Ibid. 38 (Bar-On).

[68] Richard K. Thorndike, *Intelligence and Its Uses*, Harper's Magazine 140, 1920, pp. 227-335.

[69] David Wechsler, *Nonintellective Factors in General Intelligence*, Psychological Bulletin 37, 1940, pp. 444-445.

[70] Ibid. 15 (Gardner).

[71] Ibid. 39 (Salovey & Mayer).

[72] Ibid. 40 (Goleman).

[73] Ibid. 66 (Mayer & Salovey).

[74] Ibid. 38 (Bar-On).

[75] Peter Salovey, John D. Mayer, and David R. Caruso, *"Mayer-Salovey-Caruso Emotional Intelligence Test (MSCEIT),"* Multi-Health Systems, 2002.

[76] Richard E. Boyatzis, Daniel Goleman, Kenneth Rhee, *"Clustering competence in emotional intelligence: Insights from the Emotional Competence Inventory (ECI)s"* In Reuven Bar-On and James D. A. Parker (eds.), *Handbook of emotional intelligence*, Jossey-Bass 2000, pp. 343-362.

[77] Reuven Bar-On, *"The Bar-On Model of Emotional-Social Intelligence (ESI)"* Psicothema 17, 2005, pp. 1-29.

[78] David C. McClelland, *"Testing for Competence rather than for 'Intelligence'"*, American Psychologist 28(1) 1973, pp. 1-14.

[79] Reuven Bar-On, *"The Bar-On Model of Emotional Intelligence: A valid, Robust and Applicable EI model"*, Organizations and People 14, 2007, pp. 27-34.

[80] Richard E. Boyatzis, *The Competent Manager: A Model for Effective Performance*, John Wiley and Sons, 1982.

[81] Hay/McBer Research and Innovation Group (1997). Reported by Daniel Goleman in his book – Goleman, D.; *Working with Emotional Intelligence*, New York: Bantam, 1998.

[82] David C. McClelland, *"Identifying Competencies with Behavioral Event Interviews"*, Psychological Science 9(5), 1998, pp. 331-339.

[83] Cary Cherniss and Daniel Goleman, *"The Emotionally Intelligent Workplace: How to Select For, Measure, and Improve Emotional Intelligence in Individuals, Groups, and Organizations"*,

Wiley, 2001.

[84] Carolyn Saarni, "*The development of Emotional Competence: Pathways for Helping Children to Become Emotionally Intelligent*", in R. Bar-On, J. G. Maree, & M. J. Elias (eds.), *Educating people to be emotionally intelligent*, Praeger 2007, pp. 15-36.

[85] Steven Stein, *Make Your Workplace Great: The 7 Keys to an Emotionally Intelligent Organization*, Jossey-Bass, 2007.

[86] Ibid. 49 (Keller and Price).

[87] Ibid. 48 (Barsh, Cranston and Lewis).

[88] Ibid. 49 (Keller and Price).

[89] Sonja Lyubomirsky, *The How of Happiness: A New Approach to Getting the Life You Want*, Penguin Group US, 2007.

[90] Martin Seligman, *Learned Optimism: How to Change Your Mind and Your Life*, Random House, 1990.

[91] Ibid. 12 (Garman & Dye).

[92] Ibid. 52 (Csikszentmihalyi).

www.ingramcontent.com/pod-product-compliance
Lightning Source LLC
Chambersburg PA
CBHW051443170526
45166CB00001B/98